Do not worry about
anything, but pray and
ask God for everything
you need, always
giving thanks.

PHILIPPIANS 4:6 NCV

THE 100
MOST IMPORTANT
BIBLE VERSES
FOR MOTHERS

Presented to:

_____

Presented by:

_____

Date:

_____

We also have joy with our troubles, because we know that these troubles produce patience. And patience produces character, and character produces hope. And this hope will never disappoint us, because God has poured out his love to fill our hearts.

ROMANS 5:3–5 NCV

THE 100
MOST IMPORTANT
BIBLE VERSES
FOR MOTHERS

THOMAS NELSON
Since 1798

For other products and live events,
visit us at: **thomasnelson.com**

The 100 Most Important Bible Verses for Mothers
© 2006 by GRQ, Inc.
Brentwood, Tennessee

Published in Nashville, Tennessee, by Thomas Nelson, Inc

W Publishing Group books may be purchased in bulk for educational, business, fund-raising, or sales promotional use. For information, please e-mail SpecialMarkets@ThomasNelson.com.

Scripture quotations are from the following sources:

• The New Century Version® (NCV). Copyright © 1987, 1988, 1991 by Word Publishing, a Division of Thomas Nelson, Inc. Used by permission. All rights reserved. • The New King James Version® (NKJV), copyright © 1979, 1980, 1982, Thomas Nelson, Inc., Publishers. • New Living Translation (NLT), copyright © 1996 by Tyndale House Publishers, Inc., Wheaton, Ill. All rights reserved. • The Message (MSG), copyright © 1993. Used by permission of NavPress Publishing Group.

Managing Editor: Lila Empson
Associate Editor: Laura Kendall
Manuscript: Barb Albert
Design: Thatcher Design, Nashville, Tennessee

Library of Congress Cataloging-in-Publication Data

100 most important Bible verses for mothers.
         p. cm.
Includes bibliographical references and index.
ISBN-10: 0-8499-0031-X
ISBN-13: 978-0-8499-0031-0
1. Mothers — Religious life. 2. Christian life — Biblical teaching 3. Bible — Quotations.
I. Title: One hundred most important Bible verses for mothers. II. W Publishing Group.
BV4529.18.A15 2006
220.5′2 — dc22

Printed in China
08 09 — 9 8 7 6 5

The LORD your God . . . will rejoice over you with gladness, He will quiet you with His love, He will rejoice over you with singing.

ZEPHANIAH 3:17 NKJV

Contents

Everything that was written in the past was written to teach us. The Scriptures give us patience and encouragement so that we can have hope

ROMANS 15:4 NCV

Introduction

Reading the entire Bible sounds like an overwhelming activity, one that would be difficult to make part of a day already teeming with responsibilities of home and family. No other book, however, speaks to your life as a mother like the Bible. The Bible, from start to finish, tells God's story, and that story involves you and your children in a relevant way. Your life has purpose and hope in God's story. That is encouraging.

The 100 Most Important Bible Verses for Mothers was created to give you bite-size selections from the Bible. Each selection or verse gives you wisdom for your life and guidance in matters most important to you. When you read more about the story behind each verse and the context in which it was written, you will gain a deeper understanding that will be life-changing for you and your family.

While single verses alone cannot fully express the heart and meaning contained in each chapter of the Bible, these verses give you an overview of the love message God has to share. Reading *The 100 Most Important Bible Verses for Mothers* will encourage you and give you the confidence to know where to go in the Bible when you need strength, wisdom, and peace in any aspect of your life. May *The 100 Most Important Bible Verses for Mothers* help you gain hope and joy as you experience more of God and his thoughts for you.

Those who trust in riches will be ruined, but a good person will be healthy like a green leaf.

PROVERBS 11:28 NCV

How Much Is Too Much?

Years ago, children's books, like *The Prince and the Pauper*, often featured spoiled, rich children as characters who learned through a series of hard knocks that it is better to be a poor person who is good than to be a rich one who is poor in spirit. Those charming, old-fashioned books illustrate a key to healthy, happy living. A verse in Proverbs 11 succinctly describes the same idea, giving good reason and strong motivation for refusing to rely on material things.

You want everything for your children, but that dream can prevent them from growing into well-balanced and

well-equipped adults. If children learn to look to their prosperity for comfort and security, they grow up stunted, with their focus on themselves. If they depend on the things they own, they cannot experience the true happiness that God planned for them.

> If your children learn to love God and follow his ways, they will be mature and content.

You wish for your children to grow up the best they can be. Picture them shooting up, like thriving green plants, strong and vigorous. Train them to trust completely in God for all things, for he is like the trellis around which their tender shoots wrap. Your training and love give them support to grow. Whether they have much or little, if your children learn to love God and follow his ways, they will be mature and content. Doing this when they are young will help them live good lives as adults, rich in spirit.

Teach your children to trust in God and his ways. They will grow up content and wise when they depend fully on God.

The LORD your God in your midst, the Mighty One, will save; He will rejoice over you with gladness, He will quiet you with His love, he will rejoice over you with singing.

ZEPHANIAH 3:17 NKJV

You Are Accepted

Look in the mirror. Who do you see? Do you see Jonathon and Ashley's mom, or do you see the woman you were before children? How often when you look in the mirror are you unsure who you are and too tired to care? Being a mom means losing sight sometimes of who you are when you get lost in laundry, tight schedules, and the needs of the children you love.

Your children count on your love and acceptance because you know the importance of nurturing their growing self-images. As a mother, you also need to nurture your own self-image and sense of self. As you look after yourself, you will find the strength to face the high spots and the low places of life, and the best source of acceptance is God. Zephaniah 3 is a beautiful reminder of how tenderly God views you.

God knows every part of you and your thoughts and desires in complete detail.

God has a clear picture of *you*. God is present. He looks and sees you as the one he carefully created inside your mother. God knows every part of you and your thoughts and desires in complete detail. Like everything God created, he sees whom he created and says, "It is good!" Picture the Creator of the universe thinking of you and whooping with joy. He sings in delight over the unique and special you he created. He wants to cradle you in his arms of love and, in those moments of quiet, to show his joy in you.

~ml⊚

God accepts and deeply loves you, just as you are today. Feel secure and rest in that love.

He [God] has put his angels in charge of you to watch over you wherever you go. They will catch you in their hands so that you will not hit your foot on a rock.

PSALM 91:11–12 NCV

Angels Watching Over Me

"Now I lay me down to sleep . . ." Children's prayers at bedtime sing with sweet simplicity. Young ones contentedly nestle in their beds, covered over with the assurance that God keeps them safe throughout the night. Peacefully asleep, they represent trust in a most basic way. They somehow know God's angels work to keep them safe, and believe it every time they lay their heads on their pillows, so nothing disturbs them.

When you lay your head on your pillow at night, peace can be harder to find. Thoughts from the day and concerns about the children, your job, and your relationships all swirl around in the dark of night, and it is hard to let them go. Your mind will not always settle into a quiet place when you worry about things. Peace can elude you in the daytime for the same reasons.

In Psalm 91, God reassures you with a wonderfully reassuring promise. Not only does he love and care for you, but he has entrusted his angels for your physical care and protection, day and night. These beings who serve the living God are empowered to watch over you through every circumstance you

God has entrusted his angels for your physical care and protection.

face. They are God's representatives, to carry out the things God wants to do in your life. It's a good feeling to know that they are hard at work, even when you cannot see them.

Rest in childlike faith that God's angels are on the job for you at all times, protecting you and working God's power in your life.

Think about the things that are good and worthy of praise. Think about the things that are true and honorable and right and pure and beautiful and respected.

PHILIPPIANS 4:8 NCV

What's on Your Mind?

You are what you think. You know the things you think about, read, and view affect you. If you spend much time with someone who talks coarsely, you find yourself saying some of the same things. When you view commercials promoting pizza and potato chips, you eat when you are not hungry. When you read romances and popular fashion magazines, you become discontented with your life and your children in light of the impossible standards you read. Even children's behavior becomes more aggressive when children repeatedly view violent television shows and games.

As a mom, your emotions follow the things you think about the most. When you take offense at someone's words or actions and continue to roll it over in your mind, you continue your angry feelings. Unforgiveness and bitterness may follow. Any offense entertained in your mind becomes larger than life and prevents you from following God's way of resolving problems.

Philippians 4:8 gives the best prescription to prevent bitterness and ugly feelings. God tells you how to safeguard your mind, and how to become a more positive and loving person. The same tactics also safeguard your children's minds and hearts if you teach them God's way. To stay positive, loving,

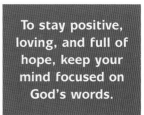

> To stay positive, loving, and full of hope, keep your mind focused on God's words.

and full of hope, keep your mind focused on God's words. The things he says are good. Do not harbor unforgiveness, anger, or bitterness. Control the influences around you and your children, including what you read and watch on television, and watch your lives bloom with more peace, love, and joy.

~◉

Fill your minds and hearts with only the best, and gain a great reward of peace, love, and joy.

There is no authority except from God, and the authorities that exist are appointed by God.

ROMANS 13:1 NKJV

The Authority God Puts in Place

"It's not fair! Why do I have to quit playing now?" You have heard statements like this many times. At every stage of growth, your children will question authority, at home first, and then at school and at work. It is human nature. Children argue whether things are fair or not, and they try to understand the way the world works from what you teach them. As they become older, the teenage years can be intense in your household if your teens cross into rebellious behavior.

Many children who become rebels begin with a real desire to right injustice in the world. God himself cares passionately about injustices of any kind. He cares for the homeless, the mistreated, the abused. He cares about wars and unjust governments. But he also set up the system of authority in heaven and on earth to work out his perfect plan for people. All authority everywhere is assigned by God.

It is crucial to teach your children how God's authority works. Make sure they learn on a firm foundation of obedience—both to God and to their parents. Teach them the importance of authority in the church, the family, and in the community, and the importance of honoring God by respecting and praying for their leaders. Show them ways to pray for and help those who cannot help themselves. In doing so, you will teach your children to love others and to love justice.

> **Many children who become rebels begin with a real desire to right injustice in the world.**

Love justice, but teach your children to respect God's appointed authorities. You honor and please God by humbly working his way.

Your beauty should come from within you—the beauty of a gentle and quiet spirit that will never be destroyed and is very precious to God.

1 PETER 3:4 NCV

Beauty Is As Beauty Does

Each day, you choose how you appear to others. Your clothing, your makeup, and your demeanor lend an impression of your identity. What motivates your choices? You are a mother of children, but all around you, the focus is on physical beauty and on admiration of the images of perfection that few can attain. Images of beautiful people sell appliances, makeup, clothing, and cars, and too often, women feel pressured to conform to them.

You sense the pressure to conform everywhere—in the workplace, in the media, even from other women in your church. Your children sense the expectations around them. Young girls believe they must dress up-to-date, use makeup, or be thinner. Some girls believe that relationships depend on a standard of outward beauty and feel lost if they are not "pretty" enough.

If you take care of yourself and your appearance, you compliment the way God made you.

If you take care of yourself and your appearance, you compliment the way God made you. It is good to cultivate any gift from him. However, the words in 1 Peter 3 illuminate the meaning of true beauty, which is cultivated inside you. True beauty lasts, and it shines through to touch the lives of those around you. You cultivate that forever beauty by loving God and letting him mature and grow you. God continually works inside you to make a woman with a gentle and quiet spirit who radiates his love. This is the beauty lesson to teach your daughters, and the standard to pass on to your sons.

What is on the outside can fade, but beauty on the inside lasts forever. Cultivate that inner beauty in you and your daughters.

Don't you see that children are GOD's best gift? the fruit of the womb his generous legacy?

PSALM 127:3 MSG

The Greatest Blessing

As precious as children are, moms around the world have days when they want to shout, "You're driving me crazy!" Think of times when you tried to finish grocery shopping with little ones grabbing things off shelves, or when dinnertime turned into a tidal wave of spilled milk, or when bickering with your teens continued all evening.

It is easy to talk about the exasperation of raising children when you are with other moms. It is a feeling common to all, and to talk about it seems to relieve some of the stress of mothering, or at least to provide some much-needed laughter. But sometimes children overhear these discussions,

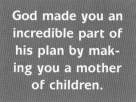

God made you an incredible part of his plan by making you a mother of children.

and if they believe they are the source of all irritation, their self-esteem plummets. More important, God always overhears these discussions.

How beautifully God reminds you what a precious blessing he gave when he allowed you to bear children or have children become a part of your life. He alone ensures generation after generation of people who will receive his promises. God made you an incredible part of his plan by making you a mother of children. Thank him for his wonderful gift, and let your children overhear how great a blessing they are to you.

—⟁—

Thank God for the incredible gift of children in your life. Don't keep it a secret! Tell your children what a blessing they are as well.

I [God] have set before you life and death, blessing and cursing; therefore choose life, that both you and your descendants may live.

DEUTERONOMY 30:19 NKJV

Choose This Day

You make hundreds of decisions every day. You choose what to feed your family, what to wear, which route to drive, and when to run errands. This is the stuff of being a mother. You run your household and keep things moving. It's hard to imagine these decisions are important to anyone but you and your family.

Deuteronomy 30:19 distinctly spells out how God looks at decisions in your life. To him they are his way or not; either black or white, life or death. You know your biggest decisions lead to life or death, but what about the myriad of smaller decisions that you face every day?

Keep God as your priority, and everything else will fall into right order.

When you set your course for life by choosing God, it means all other decisions must support life, God's life for you. God's ways and his plan all revolve around life and blessing. Your decisions for yourself and your children can too. Choose to bless with words of life in every situation. Bless your children. Speak lovingly to them even when you are frustrated. Choose jobs that allow you to have time with your family. Choose entertainment and leisure activities that God can smile on. Keep God as your priority, and everything else will fall into right order. It is possible to choose life in all things, and see your children's children blessed because of it.

Choose life in God, and your children will be blessed.

Even though on the outside it often looks like things are falling apart on us, on the inside, where God is making new life, not a day goes by without his unfolding grace.

2 CORINTHIANS 4:16 MSG

Disastrous Days

It is one of those days. You oversleep, and that brings chaos. Breakfast is a frenetic affair, and the house is a whirlwind as you rush to get things in order and find missing shoes and lunches. You work hard to get everyone where he or she needs to be that morning. Every mother experiences those days that fall apart. It is part of life with a busy family.

Whether or not the rest of the day works well, frustration can linger unless you work hard to change the way you think. Though someone watching you might think that your life is completely out of control, you have a secret on the inside that can change everything, even on those tough days.

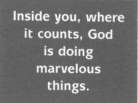

Inside you, where it counts, God is doing marvelous things.

Powerfully, you are reminded in 2 Corinthians to take the right focus. Somewhere in the midst of days that look disastrous, as well as those that are uneventful, is the truth: inside you, where it counts, God is doing marvelous things. God is washing you in a flood of grace that's yours for the taking. He wants you to call on him, in the middle of messes, and ask for the grace that allows you to take a breath and see his heavenly purpose and help. That alone will change a day full of frustration into a chance to see God making good come out of all things.

Breathe in the grace of God when life is most aggravating, and know he gives new beginnings every day when you ask.

Let your "Yes" be "Yes," and your "No," "No." For whatever is more than these is from the evil one.

MATTHEW 5:37 NKJV

Keeping Your Promises

Broken promises leave an impression. You can probably remember a time as a child when your father or mother promised something you anxiously anticipated, but for some reason it never happened. It broke your heart. Inside your heart lies a little splinter that still jabs when you remember the promise that never came true. You may have promised your own child something you could not carry through, and you know it hurts.

God's kingdom stands on irrevocable promises. In the Old Testament, people who made vows could lose their lives if they broke their promises. God's own vow, or covenant, secured your eternal salvation. His word is sacred and unbreakable. When he promised to save people from sin and death, it

Ask God for the strength to keep the promises you make.

was a done deal. God, whose words spoke life into existence and eternity into the hearts of people, takes seriously any words spoken as vows and commitments.

In your dealings with your children and others, God clearly warns you to be cautious when making promises. In Matthew 5:37, it is boiled down to its essence—make your yes, yes and your no, no. Count the cost before you speak any commitment, promise your child something, or take on a new responsibility. At every level, allow God to lead your decisions and prompt your words. Ask God for the strength to keep the promises you make, to prevent leaving behind any broken hearts.

Take every promise and vow you make seriously. Let God help you promise carefully and follow through with your word.

Keep a clear conscience so that those who speak evil of your good life in Christ will be made ashamed.

1 Peter 3:16 NCV

Free from Blame

Relationships in your family, in church, or in other places where you interact with the parents of other children take effort to keep healthy. Gossip and conflicts with others can wreck those relationships. A poorly chosen word or spreading juicy gossip about others causes trouble that bursts into flames as quickly as a forest fire, often trapping you with your own words or deeds. You endure tears, sleepless nights, and an anxious heart until others forget or until the situation resolves.

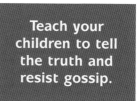

God's counsel in 1 Peter provides you with the only way to free yourself from interpersonal conflicts before they damage your relationships. You can do nothing directly to protect your own good name and reputations, any more than you can make others like you. What you can do is follow God's ways by obeying his words. He knows how to protect those who belong to him.

Teach your children to tell the truth and resist gossip.

God's words warn you to keep your own conscience clear. Resist gossip, or the urge to pass on information you have heard about others, no matter how exciting. Do not participate or enjoy listening to others speak badly of people or of others' children. Try not to lie or misrepresent the truth, and do not allow yourself to be stuck in untruths. Teach your children to tell the truth and resist gossip. By watching your own behavior, you allow God to defend you when trouble comes.

Keep yourself free from any fault by gossip or careless words and watch God defend you in the midst of trouble.

I have learned to be satisfied with the things I have and with everything that happens.

PHILIPPIANS 4:11 NCV

A Contented Woman

Contentment catches your attention. Cats lounging on the back of sofas, grandmothers rocking blissfully on the front porch, children happily playing with toys—the images of contentment stand out because they are counter to the way most people live. Paul stated that you can learn to live completely satisfied in any circumstance. How *do* you experience real contentment as a mother, with your own children, with your husband, or with your possessions?

One way to learn contentment is through your relationship with God. If you have learned to trust him, your relationship provides stability, and you can believe that anything that happens will ultimately bring you closer to him. Losses or hard times with your children turn into opportunities for God to do good things in your life. Great contentment comes from not worrying about tomorrow.

Another way contentment grows is when you trust that all your needs as a mother are provided for by God. Because the Bible promises that God will meet all your needs, you know that he will do it. If you don't have

> **Losses or hard times with your children turn into opportunities for God to do good things in your life.**

something you think you need, take it to him in prayer. Let him change your desires for your children if your desires aren't in line with God's. Let him teach you to fill up your heart with his love and grace so you can rest in beautiful contentment with your life. See your children and your surroundings as part of God's perfect plan, and thank him for it.

Be thankful and content with all that you have and all that comes into your life, and live a life God can bless.

Everything that was written in the past was written to teach us. The Scriptures give us patience and encouagement so that we can have hope.

ROMANS 15:4 NCV

Have I [the LORD] not commanded you?
Be strong and of good courage; do not be
afraid, nor be dismayed, for the LORD your
God is with you wherever you go.

JOSHUA 1:9 NKJV

You Are Courageous

When you think of courage, you picture soldiers facing the battlefront, or someone battling a serious disease. But as a mom, realize that it also takes fearlessness to raise a child. You shape the life of a human being who will eventually shape another generation of lives. The brave stand against popular opinion, and they raise children who are moral and upright followers of God. The brave do not take the easy way through life.

In day-to-day living, it takes strength on the inside to say that you are a stay-at-home mom and to shed any guilt you may feel. It takes courage to say that you are a working mom and to shed any guilt from that. Motherhood is the most important job on earth—raising part of the next generation of people to live on the earth. Every decision you make takes courage to carry through.

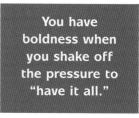

You have boldness when you shake off the pressure to "have it all."

You have boldness when you shake off the pressure to "have it all." You are resolute when you decide your children will be public-schooled, private-schooled, or homeschooled. Opinions from friends or family may counter the choices you make for your children. In the midst of all this pressure, God promises that he is going with you, leading you, giving you strength, helping you do what he calls you to do. Be strong, Mom, be strong. God has called you, and he will not leave you when the going gets tough.

Stand with fortitude and be strong. God goes with you wherever you go, helping you through every kind of pressure and decision.

He will swallow up death forever, and the Lord GOD will wipe away tears from all faces.

ISAIAH 25:8 NKJV

Death Is Not the End

You probably remember times when you had to hold a solemn assembly for the passing of a child's pet goldfish or hamster. Whether a quick prayer and a flush, or a backyard burial with songs, you know that children grieve their small pets. You try to comfort your child, though you know that even as she weeps, she will be fine in a day or so.

When beloved family members or friends die, children grieve deeply as you do. The only way to comfort them is by teaching them the truth that gives you hope from Isaiah 25. Believing and thanking God that he completely broke the power of death will sustain you in your grief and will help you comfort your child. Even though it hurts deeply, you know that death is only temporary.

God will comfort you and your children and bring healing when death comes.

Carelessness, sin, disease, and many other things end the lives of young and old. Death is part of the reality of life. God will comfort you and your children and bring healing when death comes, but he also has a forever place for you all to spend with him. Death hurts now, but you and your family can rest in the assurance that the day is coming when God will wipe away every tear.

Proclaim to your children that God is the answer to death. He defeated death and will give joy forever with him in heaven.

Delight yourself also in the LORD, and He shall give you the desires of your heart.

PSALM 37:4 NKJV

What Is in Your Heart?

Even before they were born, you started dreaming and planning for your children's future, and your dreams keep building. Your heart is full of the many things you want for them: you want them to be happy people, to grow to know God, to mature and become successful, responsible adults. Other wishes remain tucked away, and you might not even talk about them. You want so much for your children that at times your heart aches.

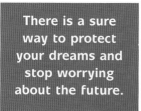

You might try to bring about those cherished dreams and hopes through your own efforts, but those efforts can be frustrated. Things sometimes go differently from the way you hope and plan. Your dreams may take on different forms as your children go. There is a sure way to protect your dreams and stop worrying about the future.

In a tender yet crystal-clear promise, Psalm 37 states that there is a wonderful way to ensure that your hopes are realized: satisfy yourself first with God, and then he will see to the wonderful hopes tucked away in your heart. When you concentrate on loving God and letting him complete you as a person, you learn to trust him more and more. In that trust, you allow God to work in the lives of your precious children. That is when you will see the desires you have for them bloom into being.

> **There is a sure way to protect your dreams and stop worrying about the future.**

Trust God with the deepest dreams of your heart and devote yourself to him. Be happy in God, for it is the best thing you can do for yourself and your children.

I do not mean that I am already as God wants me to be. I have not yet reached that goal, but I continue trying to reach it and to make it mine. Christ wants me to do that, which is the reason he made me his.

PHILIPPIANS 3:12 NCV

The Journey to Maturity

When I grow up, I want to be a . . . Remember your dreams of who you would be when you grew up? You may have wanted to be a teacher, a ballerina, or a doctor. Everything seemed possible when you were a child. Maybe you became that childhood dream. Chances are, whatever stage of life you have reached, you still wonder when you will finally "become."

As a follower of God, you have read in the Bible and been taught about what you are supposed to be—mature, growing in Christ, holy, and increasing in character, all things that sound difficult to do. As a mother, you are busy with the needs of your household and work. It's easy to feel that you are not doing enough to be where God wants you.

God's goal for you is reachable. In Philippians, Paul understands the struggle and encourages you to accept where you are and trust where God will take you. God knows the uniqueness of your life and how to perfectly implement his plan for you. Think of God's plan as a travel adventure to a new and enjoyable place. When you pray for his help, God helps you along the way. Just like traveling, you will enjoy the sights on the way. There will be bumps and detours at times, but your success lies in knowing that you are determined to go on with this journey. Keep moving in the right direction. He will lead you. You will travel to spiritual maturity as a mother with his help.

Think of God's plan as a travel adventure to a new and enjoyable place.

In God's eyes, you are on your way. He has a plan and a route for you to travel in life, so pray and ask him to show you the way.

We also have joy with our troubles, because we know that these troubles produce patience. And patience produces character, and character produces hope. And this hope will never disappoint us, because God has poured out his love to fill our hearts.

ROMANS 5:3–5 NCV

Content Despite Difficulty

Trouble comes to every mom, and when it does, you may be hard-pressed to be very happy about it. Difficulties always pop up at unexpected times, and never at good times. In Romans 5, Paul said that those wearisome periods are good, so good, in fact, that you should be delighted when they come. When you think of the last stressful time you endured with your children, you probably do not remember experiencing delight on the way through it.

The verses in Romans do more than simply advise you to be happy when you have problems. They describe a beneficial chain reaction that happens when you do. God promises to use the very trouble that vexes you to help you endure, and then to develop character within you. Character is what you are made of on the inside, and it is what you want your children to develop.

God promises to use the very trouble that vexes you to help you endure.

Imagine each time you deal with hard circumstances that your character muscles are flexing. You will find yourself encouraged as these challenges come, and better able to deal with what life brings when you realize it will ultimately make you a better person. Your children will benefit by your developing character as they see examples of maturity you set. In that whole process, God pours more and more of his love on you as you accept his purpose in the trouble that comes your way.

Don't panic when hard times come. Know that with God's help you are becoming a finer person of character, and your children will learn from what they see.

A person who does not have the Spirit does not accept the truths that come from the Spirit of God. That person thinks they are foolish and cannot understand them, because they can only be judged to be true by the Spirit.

1 CORINTHIANS 2:14 NCV

When to Speak

An old adage says no one should ever argue religion or politics. As someone who is raising children, you may not remember the last time you had a serious discussion with an adult, but tucked into that quaint saying lies wisdom from the Bible that applies to everyone, including you as a mother.

Stated in a different way, 1 Corinthians 2:14 warns that it is not possible for someone to understand God's truths unless he or she first has a close connection to God through his Spirit. This includes your children and others to whom you talk. Even though you know how precious faith is, you can't argue anyone else into believing until he or she is ready to hear it. You may have tried before to share your beliefs and been met with frustration.

> **It is not possible for someone to understand God's truths unless he or she first has a close connection to God through his Spirit.**

Sometimes people have a hard time believing God and his ways. If you understand this, you'll relieve yourself of the need to convince them. Pray for your children and others to be ready to hear and understand God's truths. Pray that they will be open to God and to what he has to say. Pray that God's Spirit will help them be ready to hear, and that when the time is right, God's Spirit will guide you to say what will help them understand.

～～

Pray for your children and their faith. Instead of arguing your beliefs, ask and wait until God shows you the right time to talk.

Get along with each other, and forgive each other. If someone does wrong to you, forgive that person because the Lord forgave you.

COLOSSIANS 3:13 NCV

Forgive and Forget

When your children have been fighting, you want them to be able to kiss and make up quickly. When it comes to forgiving people who have offended you, however, making up might be a bit harder. But there is a compelling reason for letting go of offenses quickly every time they arise. This truth will set you free from hurts that would cause you to be bitter and gives you a way to model freedom for your children.

Forgiving others starts a cycle of good things in your life. God pardoned you first for the things you had done wrong before you decided to follow him. After that, when you rethink of how he released you from guilt, know that you are to release others in the same way. God's forgiveness of you sets you free, and your forgiveness of others continues that freedom. And the cycle goes on.

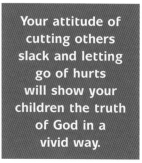

Your attitude of cutting others slack and letting go of hurts will show your children the truth of God in a vivid way.

Teach your children the power of letting offenses go. At the same time, make sure that you practice it. Your attitude of cutting others slack and letting go of hurts will show your children the truth of God in a vivid way. They will learn to forgive in their own situations and will be able to enjoy the cycle of freedom God provides. Teach your children to pray to God and forgive others as you do; blessings will come to all of you.

Release offenses, let go, and enjoy the freedom God gives to those who refuse to hold grudges.

The people who trust the LORD will become strong again. They will rise up as an eagle in the sky; they will run and not need rest; they will walk and not become tired.

ISAIAH 40:31 NCV

Energy Source

Mothers know exhaustion. You love great days when excitement with your family carries you effortlessly, but days also come when you do so much for everyone else in the family that you do not sit down until day's end. You sink into your chair after the children are in bed and realize how bone-tired you are. Some moms even wake in the morning already tired from having short sleep or from getting up during the night with a new baby or fussy toddler.

You must be cautious, because fatigue often ushers in discouragement. Looking at an endless mountain of laundry can dishearten you a bit, but physical tiredness also saps your spiritual energy and enthusiasm as well. When you do not have the momentum to spend time praying or reading the Bible, your spiritual "tank" begins to run dry, and your usual resilience wanes.

The words in Isaiah bring great news and the sweetest promise for mothers of children.

The words in Isaiah bring great news and the sweetest promise for mothers of children. God promises that if you come to him in prayer, and lay out your need and your fatigue, he will give you strength to rise above the demands of your life. God will provide what you cannot and will enable you to endure what you need in order to care for your family. That is a promise to hang on to!

When you are just too tired to make it, call on God to bring you strength. He will infuse you with fresh reserves from his endless source.

This is eternal life: that people know you, the only true God, and that they know Jesus Christ, the One you sent.

JOHN 17:3 NCV

Live by Your Bottom Line

What is your family's bottom line? What belief is at the heart of everything you do with your children? Unless you have given it serious thought, you may not know. Any group or organization operates best from a clear mission statement that keeps all activities focused and consistent. Your family, too, needs to operate from a strongly held truth, so that you teach your children to have purposeful, consistent lives.

John 17 takes powerful words of truth and states them in a dynamic bottom line that will bless and direct the lives of you and your family. Every story of the Bible, every character who struggled with faith and deeds, and every historic image depicted in God's Book all come back to this truth: forever life depends on belief in the one true God.

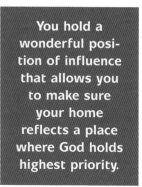

You hold a wonderful position of influence that allows you to make sure your home reflects a place where God holds highest priority.

As a mother, you hold a wonderful position of influence that allows you to make sure your home reflects a place where God holds highest priority. You can see when other things like entertainment or busyness is moving God out of first place in your family. By praying and watching out for that balance, you reinforce in your children the importance of knowing God. Your home will beautifully reflect what makes God happy, and your children will grow up knowing what the bottom line should always be in their lives.

Watch out for your family, and keep God first in all you do. Your children will learn to follow him all their lives because of the example you set for them.

Love your enemies. Pray for those who hurt you. If you do this, you will be true children of your Father in heaven. He causes the sun to rise on good people and on evil people, and he sends rain to those who do right and to those who do wrong.

MATTHEW 5:44–45 NCV

The Good and the Bad

Your children know there are good people and bad people in the world. You teach them to trust some people and to be careful around anyone else. It is part of living in today's world. Sometimes your child comes home from school crying because someone acted mean to her, and you become upset and angry. You want to let the other child's parents know just how badly their child acted. God has a better response for you than getting angry and reacting. You can practice and teach your children the response that will give them a place of peace when someone hurts them.

There is only one response God wants from you when you are mistreated. You already pray for people you care for. Those prayers flow easily. It is harder to pray for those who do mean things to your family, or who make life difficult for you. No matter if the trouble is small or more serious, God still asks the same thing of you as a first

God asks you to love even difficult people by praying for his blessing and will for them.

response. Pray. Pray for those who have hurt you. This pleases God, eases your stress, and makes you a more joyful person.

Everything God does has purpose. God asks you to love even difficult people by praying for his blessing and will for them. You must teach yourself and your children to pray for all people and so allow God to work his purpose in their lives. By doing this, your children will learn how to deal with hurts.

Pray for all people, even those who cause you harm. When you let go of any offense, you allow God to work in the lives of the offenders and bless them.

God can do anything, you know—far more than you could ever imagine or guess or request in your wildest dreams!

EPHESIANS 3:20 MSG

No Limit with God

Your children love superheroes and fantastic stories. They believe anything is possible. In their young hearts, men can fly with a cape, dogs can talk and help people, and rainbows may actually taste like cotton candy. Their hearts are unlimited by doubt about anything, and they need your careful guidance as they grow and learn about the world around them.

Your children also believe more of the truth about God than many logic-minded adults do. Can God move mountains? Can he make day night and night day? Can he heal sick bodies and make dead people alive again? Did Jesus feed five thousand people with just a little bit of bread and fish? Of course! Children believe it simply because the Bible says it is so. Belief is easy for them.

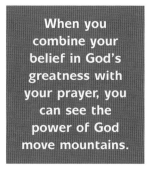

When you combine your belief in God's greatness with your prayer, you can see the power of God move mountains.

God gives you permission to respond freely as a child. He challenges you to loosen up your idea of who he is and what he can do. In effect, he says to you today, "Take away the box you've put me in, and open your mind to believe once again that anything is possible." When you combine your belief in God's greatness with your prayer, you can see the power of God move mountains. Let God be who he is, the glorious Creator and limitless God of all that you can see.

With praise in your heart, approach God with belief in his limitless ability to answer prayer in amazing ways. You will see it in your life and the lives of your children.

Without faith no one can please God. Anyone who comes to God must believe that he is real and that he rewards those who truly want to find him.

HEBREWS 11:6 NCV

Please God and Just Believe

In the story of Winnie-the-Pooh, Eeyore the Donkey loved to moan to everyone that no matter what, good things would just never happen for him. If the sun shone on his picnic, he remained convinced a thunderstorm had to be coming. The poor stuffed donkey had no faith, and his groaning made your children laugh when they heard the story.

You may sometimes feel like Eeyore as a follower of God, and find it hard to believe that God always has good planned for you and your family's lives. The words in Hebrews 11 warn clearly that lack of faith in God's eyes is not as adorable as the charming pessimism of the storybook character. Doubt in God and in his goodness is the only force on earth that can stop him from doing his will.

To follow God, believe he exists. When you go to him in prayer and for fellowship, believe that he wants to bless you, that he wants to answer your prayers, and that he wants to reward you for your diligence in searching for more of him. Believe also that he is in control and that whatever happens, he is standing at the helm of the universe. To rest in that faith and release doubt puts you and your family in a place of God's pleasure and blessing.

> God always has good planned for you and your family's lives.

Believe and stand unshakable in your faith, no matter the circumstances that come your way, and you will be blessed because you love and trust God.

The people who trust the LORD will become strong again. They will rise up as an eagle in the sky; they will run and not need rest; they will walk and not become tired.

ISAIAH 40:31 NCV

Each one of you must love his wife as he loves himself, and a wife must respect her husband. Children, obey your parents as the Lord wants, because this is the right thing to do.

EPHESIANS 5:33—6:1 NCV

The Perfect Family

God designed families, and he designed the way families work. In his perfect plan, described in the detailed blueprint in Ephesians 5, he asks husbands and wives each to love selflessly, and together, as parents, to teach their children to obey God. When children obey God, his plan is to bless them and their future.

You can see that this is a most effective way to raise emotionally healthy children. When mutual respect and self-

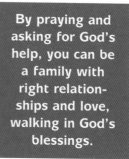
lessness flow through the family, God can hold top priority, and each family member can receive what he or she needs spiritually and emotionally. God, however, does not limit his blessing to perfect family configurations. He knows that not every family has all the elements needed to fit the ideal plan. Because he is God, he has a plan to cover that fact.

> By praying and asking for God's help, you can be a family with right relationships and love, walking in God's blessings.

Wherever you are as a family, you can start there. If you are a single mother, you can have respect for your children and teach them to obey God. In the same way, if your spouse does not follow God, you can still show respect and love to him, but take responsibility for teaching your children to obey God. God brings healing to every part of your life. By praying and asking for God's help, you can be a family with right relationships and love, walking in God's blessings.

Be the family you are, and let God fill in any gaps! Ask him for his perfect plan for your family, and let him bless you.

God has not given us a spirit of fear, but of power and of love and of a sound mind.

2 TIMOTHY 1:7 NKJV

No Fear

Every parent experienced in crawling under beds with "monster spray" knows the power of fear. Children are afraid of things they do not understand or cannot interpret accurately. Parents are afraid of things they know and cannot change. As a mom, you will not let your children play with sharp sticks or wrestle in the yard for fear that one of them will get hurt. As the children get older, your fears become bigger. They grip your heart when a teenager is late coming home.

Fear chokes out the love of God. It keeps you from standing confidently in God's care, which produces even more fear. Fear throws off-balance the freedom your children need to grow and learn, as opposed to parental caution, which sets reasonable limits. Fear stops you from stepping into new experiences of growth for yourself.

> **Depend on the fact that God gives you power to live your life well, gives you love enough to care for your family and yourself, and gives you a healthy mind.**

Throughout the seasons of your life, your situation will continue changing, and at times, bring new issues that may cause fear. Whether you are facing the change of life, problems with your children, or uncertainties with employment, you can be free from fear. The promise in the first chapter of 2 Timothy shows you the way. God is absolutely trustworthy in every situation. Depend on the fact that God gives you power to live your life well, gives you love enough to care for your family and yourself, and gives you a healthy mind. Pray, thank God for his freedom, and believe it!

~

Trust that God does not bring fear, but that he will provide the way out of fear. Believe that truth with all your heart.

Let's see how inventive we can be in encouraging love and helping out, not avoiding worshiping together as some do but spurring each other on, especially as we see the big Day approaching.

HEBREWS 10:24–25 MSG

Take Time for Family

As a mom, you stretch time as far as it will go. You tote tots, bring home the groceries, and get everyone where they need to be. You keep the schedule of work and school running smoothly, and you stay busy. If anyone knows where all the members of the family should be at any given time, you do. At the end of a long day, you put your feet up and know that your family benefited from your hard work and creativity.

Weekend mornings may seem like a wonderful time for your family to sleep in and enjoy a few relaxing hours of downtime, but making time to attend church promises to do more for your family than a few hours of extra sleep. A much bigger family at church will love you and give you a chance to serve God and others in ways you may never have imagined.

> **Making time to attend church promises to do more for your family than a few hours of extra sleep.**

Time spent in worship with other followers of God helps your whole family grow spiritually. Hebrews 10 challenges you to be creative and find ways to bless and encourage others, even as you are blessed and encouraged in the fellowship of church. You and your family will be able to do that as you learn and grow with others. Be a part of a gathering of people who are alive and full of God's Spirit, and you will be glad for Sunday mornings!

Invest yourself in fellowship with others who love God, and reap the rewards of spiritual blessing for your whole family.

We continue to preach Christ to each person, using all wisdom to warn and to teach everyone, in order to bring each one into God's presence as a mature person in Christ.

COLOSSIANS 1:28 NCV

Raise Children for God

When it comes to sharing your faith with others, the most important place to start is in your own home. Your children want to know how to have God in their lives. They want to know how to pray and what the Bible says about living a good life. And the best teacher for them is you.

Knowing where to start teaching your children about their faith may seem to be a puzzle at first, but you know how important it is. Colossians 1 expresses the importance of sharing your faith and bringing others to a point of spiritual maturity. For you, it is your children you bring to maturity, and the most natural way to do this is to bring God into everything that happens in your life. Talk about God when good things happen, when bad things occur, or when life is joyous or tedious. Your children will learn about God in a very natural way.

As you go on, teach them God's laws and promises from the Bible, and give them chances to interact with other people who are both wise and

> You are your children's best teacher because you love them, and God will bless your efforts.

followers of God. When your children are grown, you want them to live by the values found in the Bible. God will teach them as they learn about him, and God will give you the wisdom you need. You are your children's best teacher because you love them, and God will bless your efforts.

Talk about God throughout your day. Teach your sons and daughters how to be people of faith, and help them be who God wants them to be.

Give, and you will receive. You will be given much. Pressed down, shaken together, and running over, it will spill into your lap. The way you give to others is the way God will give to you.

LUKE 6:38 NCV

Giving Freely

A fistful of squished yellow dandelions, a paper with a crooked rainbow colored on it, a heart with "I love you" penned across it—your children are naturally giving to the ones they love. They give with great delight and affection when they are young, and often would give away their own toys if you did not stop them.

Something happens as children get older. Unless cultivated, that free, giving spirit changes as the child matures and learns to look at things "reasonably" and with "good sense." Your own giving spirit might have shriveled in the face of adulthood, particularly when you faced the reality of having a family to support. Adulthood is serious business.

God's call to you is to regain the abandonment and the joy of giving. Instead of a careful measure of what you think you can do, give freely and generously. God will generously give back as freely as you give. What a promise — he will never fail you. Proclaim your faith and trust in God, and become

> God's call to you is to regain the abandonment and the joy of giving.

like a child again, believing he will do what he said he would. Imagine the people you can bless when you give with God's abandonment.

Learn to give freely and joyfully like a child again, and God will give back to you in that same measure.

Can a woman forget her nursing child, and not have compassion on the son of her womb? Surely they may forget, yet I will not forget you. See, I have inscribed you on the palms of My hands.

ISAIAH 49:15–16 NKJV

Unforgettable Love

A mother who breast-feeds her infant knows the longing she feels when her baby is hungry. She feels an ache that quickly becomes desperation to hold her baby and give him the milk he needs. She cannot ignore it, and she feels sweet relief when her baby rests in her arms. God beautifully designed the process of feeding an infant to encourage the bond of mother and child.

The Bible's use of this comparison in Isaiah 49 is stunningly clear, particularly for mothers. God can no more forget you than a mother can ignore the physical need for her infant and the deeply compelling ache in her breast to be holding that infant closely. This image takes your breath away.

The verses go on to say that your name is engraved on the palms of his hands. Picture how many times you see the palms of your hands during a day. They are ever before you. Your hands bless and touch your children in love throughout the day. Two powerful images convey a love God has for you

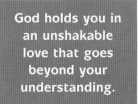

God holds you in an unshakable love that goes beyond your understanding.

that is too deep to comprehend. God holds you in an unshakable love that goes beyond your understanding. Think deeply about the words of God, and thank God in prayer for his love. You are never out of his mind, and you can walk out each day comforted by this knowledge.

God thinks tenderly about you all the time, as a loving parent. Be comforted to know that he cannot forget you for even a moment.

Arise, shine; for your light has come! And the glory of the LORD is risen upon you.

ISAIAH 60:1 NKJV

Let It Shine

"This little light of mine, I'm gonna let it shine." Like the song you sang as a child, Isaiah said your light has come. Are you shining? God's brilliance rests on you. Try to imagine what that looks like—it's almost beyond comprehension. The idea of God shining through you is as wonderful as it is hard to picture.

Think of your children as they wake in their rooms in the morning. Golden sunlight fills the room with increasing intensity and wakes them to the glorious possibilities of a new day. Their faces catch the rays of the sun and glow with the golden color. Those faces are at once delicate and incredibly alive. Now wake to the glories of God yourself. God's light shines all the time, and gives you a

God's light shines all the time, and gives you a fresh start, a new day, every day.

fresh start, a new day, every day. You can be filled with that light—as a mother, as a wife, as a woman—and have the same glow.

It is an awesome responsibility to shine the light of God on your children. Another old song says they will know you're a Christian by your love. That's God's light shining through you in ways that the world can see. Living and reflecting the intense glow of God is caught, not taught. As you allow God to shine through your life by giving yourself freely to him, your children will see and give their hearts to him as well.

A little light dispels much darkness. Give yourself to God, and let his light shine through you wherever you go.

In Your presence is fullness of joy; at Your right hand are pleasures forevermore.

PSALM 16:11 NKJV

Joy in Following God

You love your children, and they often bring you great enjoyment. When you focus on their endearing qualities, wouldn't it be nice if you could freeze time so you could keep on enjoying them? At other times, taking care of your children and seeing to their needs takes a great deal of work alongside the pleasure. That is common in most enduring relationships.

When you think of being a follower of God as a busy mom, all the praying, Bible reading, and church attendance seem like a lot of work. But here's a secret: loving God and having a relationship with him aren't supposed to be work. Loving God and having a relationship with him are meant to be incredibly delightful. Just as you enjoy the time you spend with a best friend, you can truly enjoy the company of God.

> Loving God and having a relationship with him are meant to be incredibly delightful.

You can experience God in a deep and satisfying way. As with your children, when you focus on God's amazing qualities, you will want to spend time in awe of him. In spite of your busy schedule, you can find small amounts of time to spend focusing on God every day, and in doing so you will find it is like the longing you have to spend time with your best friend. The enjoyment God promises to you will grow and make it easier to include him in each day.

Find some time to spend with God each day, and learn to relish him as a friend. He promises you will enjoy it!

$\mathbf{D}$o not change yourselves to be like the people of this world, but be changed within by a new way of thinking. Then you will be able to decide what God wants for you; you will know what is good and pleasing to him and what is perfect.

ROMANS 12:2 NCV

Easy Decisions

Every day you make decisions. Some decisions are easier to make than others, but when you make decisions that involve your children, you know each one is important. Some moms look for help in deciding which paths to take by talking to other moms, getting advice from friends, and reading books and materials that promise to make you successful in child rearing.

How do you know what to do when your decisions affect your children and your family? God never intended you to function completely on your own, making all your decisions based on your own thinking. He has a clear and definite plan for you and your family. With God a dynamic process is at work, and all things can be used for

Praying, reading the Bible, and letting God change your way of thinking transform you.

good in your life and in the lives of your children. Mom, you can plug into God's power source and receive help from God's unsurpassed wisdom for your everyday life.

What a help—assistance from the One who created everything that exists. You allow God to influence your mind when you spend time with him. Praying, reading the Bible, and letting God change your way of thinking transform you. Then you are speaking God's language, which will help you understand his purposes for you and your family.

—

Don't make decisions alone. Fill your mind with the Bible, and let God change your way of thinking to his.

God means what he says. What he says goes. His powerful Word is sharp as a surgeon's scalpel, cutting through everything, whether doubt or defense, laying us open to listen and obey. Nothing and no one is impervious to God's Word. We can't get away from it—no matter what.

HEBREWS 4:12–13 MSG

More Than Words

When was the last time you read a good book? As a mom, your reading time is probably a bit limited. By the time the day is over, you may lack the time or the energy to read for enjoyment. You'd like to make regular Bible reading part of your faith life, but sometimes it's not so easy to fit it in. Imagine, though, that you heard one particular book could amazingly change your life for the better if you read it every day. Now that's an exciting promise!

God's words are great words to read, but they're so much more. God's words tell of power and mystery in the words spoken by the Creator of the universe. These words are life-changing. The Bible says that in the beginning the Word *was* God. God is somehow present in his words, and his words have the power to do what he wants, changing your life in perfect ways.

Teach your children respect for God's words by showing that respect yourself. Read to them and cultivate their habit of reading for themselves every day. Read the Bible thoughtfully

> **When you speak the words of God about situations you face, you are speaking the power of God into them.**

and prayerfully, and it will change you. When you speak the words of God about situations you face, you are speaking the power of God into them. As you read the Bible, ask God to show you how his words can have the most meaning in your life.

God's words are more than just words. Read them, pray about them, and think about them. Watch God bring his power into your life.

All have sinned and are not good enough for God's glory, and all need to be made right with God by his grace, which is a free gift.

ROMANS 3:23–24 NCV

Freedom from Guilt

When you started your family, you might have day-dreamed about the kind of mother you wanted to be. You knew if you could just be the perfect mom, you would raise perfectly wonderful children. It was easy to set parental standards for yourself that were so high they were nearly unreachable.

Once your children arrived, you found out rather quickly that you couldn't be a perfect mother. You made mistakes. You lost your temper. You said things that you never thought you would say. Because mistakes in parenting involve the children who are so dear to your heart, they can make you feel terrible. Guilt can rob you of the joy of caring for your family if you let it.

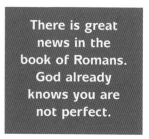

There is great news in the book of Romans. God already knows you are not perfect.

There is great news in the book of Romans. God already knows you are not perfect. Every person, even though created by God, has done wrong things and missed the mark. Thankfully, you do not have to live with the guilt of what you have done wrong. You can pray to God and tell him that you fall short as a mother, or about whatever weighs you down, and you can have the peace that comes only from him as he forgives you. Let God help you as a mom, and enjoy the freedom he gives.

Ask God to forgive anything that weighs down your heart, and he will cut you free from that weight with his rich love for you.

I will comfort you as a mother comforts her child.

ISAIAH 66:13 NCV

The Arms of God

A crying child wants nothing but her mother. You scoop her up and hold her, speaking softly and smoothing down her hair. Your arms cradle her and make her feel safe as you rock back and forth. She needs this tenderness more than anything else when she is distressed, and no one else can make her feel exactly the same way.

As a grownup, you sometimes wish you had someone to hold you like that when things go wrong and your day is horrible. Amazingly enough, you can know that kind of comfort from God. You need gentleness and tenderness that no one else but God can give you. Because God made you, he knows just what speaks to the place of your sadness or hurt. The splendid image Isaiah described compares the solace from God to the solace you give to your own child. What a great comfort. God will hold you, wipe your tears, speak words of love in your ear, and assure you that he can take care of any problem.

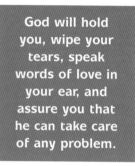

God will hold you, wipe your tears, speak words of love in your ear, and assure you that he can take care of any problem.

Isaiah spoke of a promise that God's people would be comforted. Mothers and children and everyone else need healing for the bumps and bruises of life. God sent his Spirit to bring his comfort to you when you need it. Pray, and bring your need to God and ask him to hold you in his arms.

Look to God to bring you a gentle touch when life hurts. Talk to him in prayer, and he will hold you tenderly as you trust him like a child.

Can a woman forget her nursing child, and not have compassion on the son of her womb? Surely they may forget, yet I will not forget you. See, I have inscribed you on the palms of My hands.

ISAIAH 49:15–16 NKJV

I pray that you may prosper in all things and be in health, just as your soul prospers.

3 JOHN 2 NKJV

Mind and Soul

Medical researchers talk about a mind-and-body connection in the wellness of people. Stress affects your physical soundness in complex ways, and that's why your doctor asks questions about the stress level in your life when you have a medical checkup. If you're like most moms, you might answer that you face stress every day.

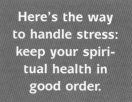

The Bible as well connects the condition of the soul with the health of the body—and did so long before science "discovered" it. Your soul touches and responds to God, and your spiritual health and your physical health are often correlated. The stress of caring for children can sometimes be great,

> Here's the way to handle stress: keep your spiritual health in good order.

and dealing with that stress can sometimes be neglected. But here's the way to handle stress: keep your spiritual health in good order.

All moms have times of feeling pressured, angry, and frustrated. God can help you know how to handle those feelings, and with his help you can grow spiritually and become a stronger and wiser mom. The key is to pray when you get perturbed and your stress levels start to rise. Ask God for help right then, and keep asking until you're calmer. Even doctors know that people who pray are healthy people, and you know the secret why!

Take your upsets to God, and ask for his help. He will bring health to all areas of your body when you depend on him.

Good people bring good things out of the good they stored in their hearts. But evil people bring evil things out of the evil they stored in their hearts. People speak the things that are in their hearts.

LUKE 6:45 NCV

When You're Squeezed

If you squeeze an orange at your breakfast table for your children, orange juice comes out, not grape juice or milk. What is inside the fruit comes out under pressure. When life squeezes you, what comes out? Pressures and troubles squeeze you, and the squeezing brings out what is inside you. You have seen this when your kids are all rais-

ing a ruckus at once and something comes out of your mouth that shocks even you.

What you say and do gives a fairly accurate picture of who you are. Onlookers won't be forced to guess. Luke explained that what lies in your heart comes out in what you say. Understand this truth— bad words are not just innocent slips of the tongue, but a reminder to call on God to change your heart.

> **Your words are a barometer to the goodness in your heart.**

Children sometimes manage to press all your buttons, and family issues will come up. Being a mom can be challenging. The stressors that you experience can bring you to a good place when they show you your need. Your words are a barometer to the goodness in your heart. Your children will flourish when your words are full of grace and gentleness, and when you pass on this truth to them.

Thwart stress. Ask God to fill your heart—and your mouth—with good so that everyday pressures bring out your true nature.

He will gather the lambs with His arm, and carry them in His bosom, and gently lead those who are with young.

ISAIAH 40:11 NKJV

The Tender Side of God

Think of what you know of little lambs—wobbly, fuzzy, and knock-kneed. They are not strong yet, no more than young kittens or puppies, and they are very vulnerable. Imagine a shepherd who takes care of the lambs, carrying them in his arms when they are too tired to keep up, or too weak to walk. A shepherd cares for every need the sheep have, including protecting the ones who are expecting young.

God is your Shepherd. His caring for you is beautiful and deep. God knows when you are particularly weak or vulnerable, when you are stressed and strained. He will lead you tenderly at those times. You may have felt you were alone and afraid at times in the past, but the truth is that he was

When you face challenging situations, God will keep you in his loving arms.

always there, just as he is now. When you are physically drained or emotionally exhausted, God nurtures you with tender care.

When you face challenging situations, God will keep you in his loving arms. Pray to God and tell him your fears and concerns, and he will keep you on a safe path, and see to all the things you need. He wants you to trust in his deep and complete compassion for you, no matter what stage of life you face. Tap into the tender side of God, and know you are safe from harm.

When you are weak, he is strong. Trust God to protect and guide you at all times, for he is compassionate toward you.

God has given us every spiritual blessing in the heavenly world. That is, in Christ, he chose us before the world was made so that we would be his holy people—people without blame before him.

EPHESIANS 1:3–4 NCV

Holy in God's Eyes

It is a good day when you go to bed and have no regrets about your day. Some nights you just want to crawl between the covers and get some sweet sleep. Your days overflow with activities and responsibilities. Your children need you in so many ways: Where are Johnny's shoes? Did Linda study for her history quiz? What would be healthy yet quick to fix for supper? And, oh dear, Laura's tap lesson . . . It's easy to feel overwhelmed, even when you know you're a good organizer.

God chose you to be his, not because of your actions and behavior, but because of your relationship with him. As a parent, you believe your children are perfectly wonderful because they are your children. So also does God feel about you, because you are *his* child. God sees your capabilities, your human-ness, and your imperfection. And he calls you "without blame."

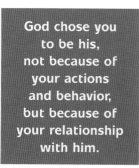

God chose you to be his, not because of your actions and behavior, but because of your relationship with him.

God continues to perfect you and change you from the inside out. And just as God sees you without blame because you are his, you should see your children in the same way. They are yours; you love them; you discipline them fairly; and you hold them without blame. See them as God sees them, righteous by position, and nurtured by you in the grace of God.

—⁂—

He has called you holy and he has called you his. Let him continue to make you perfect in his eyes.

If you then, being evil, know how to give good gifts to your children, how much more will your heavenly Father give the Holy Spirit to those who ask Him!

LUKE 11:13 NKJV

The Best Gift

How quickly you respond to your child when he truly needs something: your sick child who needs relief, your hungry child who needs lunch, your growing child who needs bigger shoes and bigger pants, your sad child who needs comfort—you don't hesitate. If it is within your power to give him what he needs, you will do it. Luke knew the strength of a mother's concern for her children, and he used a vivid illustration of this to make a point.

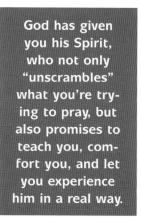

At times, it is tempting to rush in to do things by yourself rather than wait for God's answers, but when you do pray for your family and for your needs, you want to be assured that God hears your need. It is hard to know how to put into words what you need from God when you aren't always sure yourself. In ancient times, a priest prayed for the people, but today God has given you his Spirit, who not only "unscrambles" what you're trying to pray, but also promises to teach you, comfort you, and let you experience him in a real way.

> **God has given you his Spirit, who not only "unscrambles" what you're trying to pray, but also promises to teach you, comfort you, and let you experience him in a real way.**

Having God's Spirit in your life is like having a perfect gift from a loving parent. God's Spirit makes your life easier and richer. How like God to know the perfect gift for you!

Ask God to give you his Spirit, and believe you will receive. He will give you what you need to grow.

Open your homes to each other, without complaining.

1 PETER 4:9 NCV

Entertain Others Gladly

An open door to a friend's home is as welcoming as a warm hug. A cup of tea, a cozy chair, and good conversation make you feel loved. The gift of hospitality takes many forms but always pulls you into the love of God. You and your children can extend that hospitality to others, no matter where you live or what you like to do.

Hospitality extends grace to others, whether by feeding them, entertaining them, or offering a place to stay. A cheerful disposition makes others feel welcome and accepted, and it is important enough that it is described in 1 Peter 4:9. You demonstrate the love of God by reaching out and entertaining others in a way that is practical and effective. Practice hospitality gladly with open doors to guests.

You have abilities that you can use to love others practically. You may be able to host your children's friends in an atmosphere that is safe and loving in which to play, or to invite other mothers for a cup of coffee. You may be able to offer a short-term place for families who don't have a place to stay, a recipe for cookies that can put a smile on anyone's face, or a way of decorating a church basement to feel like home. God has put something in you that you can share in some way, spreading the love of God. Ask him to show you what you can do to extend his hospitality to others.

> You have abilities that you can use to love others practically.

Use the gifts you have to reach out and love others in a practical way. It does not matter how big or small the effort—it is your own.

Younger people should be willing to be under older people. And all of you should be very humble with each other. "God is against the proud, but he gives grace to the humble."

1 PETER 5:5 NCV

No Bragging Rights

It is a familiar scene—mothers at the playground chatting as they watch their children play. Too soon, someone begins boasting about her child's accomplishments in school or on the soccer field, and other mothers join in. You may even hear moms bragging about what they have or how well their husbands are doing. It is easy to get caught up in that boasting. But it's also easy to learn to appreciate the successes of other mothers' children.

God's words about puffed-up attitudes are strong in 1 Peter 5:5. It says that God is against the proud, so of course that is your goal, to turn back pride. Wear a humble attitude at all times, particularly in your dealings with other people. Be willing and able to learn from older women who have been in your shoes before.

You know your children are wonderful, and your husband is the greatest. The temptation to join in and top another person's story is strong, but think about the ones who are listening. Other moms may be quietly struggling with problems and be close to despair. Instead of bragging, seek to be a vehicle of God's grace and peace. Be thankful to God always, ask him to show you any areas of pride, and you will soon wear the humble attitude that is pleasing to God.

> **Be willing and able to learn from older women who have been in your shoes before.**

Before pride trips you up, ask God to show you where you brag and boast. He will help you become humble and joyfully dependent on him.

"The virgin shall be with child, and bear a Son, and they shall call His name Immanuel," which is translated, "God with us."

Matthew 1:23 nkjv

Everyone Loves Babies

People love babies. Most people want to hold them and talk baby talk to them. Maybe it is their size and their helplessness that are so appealing. When you see a baby, you see the hope and possibility resting in him. Babies have their whole world ahead of them, and when you look at them you smile and appreciate their potential.

In the time of Jesus, people needed a new king to come and rule in rightness and splendor. They were desperate for a new start, and for hope. What they got was a baby who had to crawl, then learn to walk, fall down, and be raised by parents who helped him learn. What an amazing way for God to send a Savior! No one expected a baby to be the answer.

The first chapter of Matthew clearly and efficiently announces the miracle of the baby. The miracle was God's Son coming in a way that people could relate to, in a form that represented hope and new beginnings. By coming as a baby and

> **Think about the amazing hope that came when one special Baby was born.**

growing into a man, Jesus could experience human growing pains, sorrows, joys, and frustrations. He went through it. When you think of the joy and hope you felt when your children were born, think about the amazing hope that came when one special Baby was born.

God's Son came as a baby—a representative of hope the whole world needed. Thank God for that blessed event.

Nothing gives me greater joy than to hear that my children are following the way of truth.

3 JOHN 1:4 NCV

Celebrate the Faith of Your Children

You celebrate all your child's achievements. You are excited when her team wins a soccer game. You chart the milestones of her first teeth, her first words, and her first steps in her baby book. Every first day of school and every graduation day means happiness for your family, and some-times justification for a party. And your children love to be at the center of your appreciation.

The Bible points out a time to celebrate in your child's life that needs to be at the top of the list: you should have greater excitement about your child following God's ways than about anything else. In terms of the achievements that dictate the course of your child's life, her commitment to God and following his ways are most important. With a strong spiritual base, your child can be better equipped for any path her life follows.

> **Place your child's spiritual development at the top of the list of things she needs.**

Place your child's spiritual development at the top of the list of things she needs. Make sure that teaching her about God gets attention before all the other things that make her a well-balanced person. When you can see she is following God's ways, have a time of celebration for the milestones of her faith. Pull out the stops, invite your family and friends, and let her know that she is doing something of the greatest value.

Let God guide you as he draws your children close to him. Then go all out in happiness when your children take big steps to follow God.

Blessed are the merciful, for they shall obtain mercy.

MATTHEW 5:7 NKJV

What You Give, You Will Receive

You teach your children that if they treat people well, they will be treated well by others. Variations of that advice have encouraged young ones to straighten up for years. You may also tell them that if they want to have a friend, they have to be a friend. This is a universal equation that children can understand: their actions have consequences that will affect their lives in significant ways.

The Bible has a key equation you must know: anyone who shows kindness and compassion to others will receive that same kindness and compassion from God. This is part of a list of blessings that God says will come from being a person who does things his way. Such an inspiring equation! You would never say that you did not want God's kindness in your life. You want what he has to give, and so you listen carefully to the conditions he spells out.

Life can be hard, raising children can be challenging, and you need all the help you can get.

You need God's kindness and compassion in your life. Life can be hard, raising children can be challenging, and you need all the help you can get. Ask God for his help, and then extend that loving goodness to people in your life. Show kindness to your children, your family, and your neighbors, and be sure to give others a break when they make mistakes. It costs you nothing to be gracious to others. If you do, you will see more and more of God's kindness given back into your life.

⁓⫯⊙

Be kind to others, and God will be kind to you. Share his love with those around you and receive a rich reward.

It takes wisdom to have a good family, and it takes understanding to make it strong.

PROVERBS 24:3 NCV

Help!

Wouldn't it be nice if raising a family came with an instruction manual? Some days you may feel that you are traveling through uncharted territory with no map or guideline. Issues with your children come up, some things you are *sure* your mother never told you about. You are not certain where your children get some of their ideas, but your heart longs to have a strong and well-balanced family.

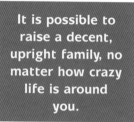

Incredibly, you *do* have a manual that helps you raise your family in a very successful way. It is the Bible. Proverbs 24:3 boils it down to two things absolutely necessary for the kind of family you want. It says you need to be wise and have understanding of God's ways in order to bring up your children. Does that sound too simple?

> **It is possible to raise a decent, upright family, no matter how crazy life is around you.**

It is possible to raise a decent, upright family, no matter how crazy life is around you. God, who created the idea of people living in loving families, knows the best ways to deal with all the issues of life. He is completely wise, as much today as he was in the beginning. With God's help, you can address the problems and challenges you face. Nothing is too big. With the ideas you have from studying the Bible, and with God's help when you pray, you can find the way to guide your family to success.

Trust the One who wrote the manual on healthy families. Read the Bible, pray for wisdom, and let God help you raise your family.

Teach your children to choose the right path, and when they are older, they will remain upon it.

PROVERBS 22:6 NLT

Each One Is Special

You know each of your children is different. You may have noticed that you cannot repeat the same actions of parenting with each child successfully because your efforts will have different results. The same method of discipline used on two different children will effectively stop one child's bad behavior, but will crush the feelings of another child. No blanket approach works as you raise your family, but that is just evidence that God designed each child to be special.

You want to train your children for adulthood, for spiritual maturity, and to be leaders in some capacity in life. Some days it seems that you are doing a lot of work for few results as you try to teach them. Even when your children are teens, they may not demonstrate the results of all your hard work, and that can be frustrating. But do not believe that you have wasted your time.

> Spend time praying for each of your children, and ask God to show you how to approach and appreciate the uniqueness of each one.

You have a strong promise that can sustain you even if it appears your work was fruitless. If you seek God for wisdom, and if you pray to know how to train each child according to the way God made him, then eventually that training will show in the child's life. Spend time praying for each of your children, and ask God to show you how to approach and appreciate the uniqueness of each one.

⟶⫯⊙

Ask God how to teach and direct your children as individuals. Do your best and trust God with the results.

We have freedom now, because Christ made us free. So stand strong. Do not change and go back into the slavery of the law.

GALATIANS 5:1 NCV

Free from Burden

Mothers put heavy loads on themselves. Expectations of perfection as parents and homemakers, wanting to raise children who are high achievers, and juggling your many responsibilities all add heavy weight to you. Those kinds of burdens can drag you down and keep you from feeling the peace of being stress-free. Unrealistic expectations can come from inside you or from other people in your life.

Guilt or regret about the way things could have been creates heaviness in your life. You may feel limitations on the kind of mother you can be because of the way you were raised, or you may struggle with areas of sin that you cannot leave behind. The good news about the back-breaking burdens you feel is this: God already made the way for you to be free from anything that holds you.

God already made the way for you to be free from anything that holds you.

God changed your life by his Son, Jesus, coming into the world. He broke forever the hold that sin and unrealistic expectations and every other heavy thing has on you. Take those things to God in prayer and leave them there. Thank God for the freedom he gave to you, and ask him daily for the strength to walk away from that heaviness and never pick it up again. Then enjoy motherhood without the heavy load.

〜𝑚〜

God made the way for you to be free. Drop the burdens that weigh you down, and be a truly liberated mom.

Listen, my child, to what your father teaches you. Don't neglect your mother's teaching. What you learn from them will crown you with grace and clothe you with honor.

PROVERBS 1:8–9 NLT

Leave the Inspiration to God

Sometimes mothers complain their children will not listen to them. This unfortunately common problem situation in families grows to greater size when the children become teens. Many believe it is inevitable for children to stop respecting their parents, and the expectation receives strong reinforcement from everything young teens see or hear from peers or the media. Disrespect is accorded social standing. That kind of opposition is tough.

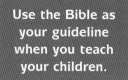

God's expectation for families is radically different. In the first chapter of Proverbs, children have a very special and very specific piece of advice with a promise attached to it. It states very clearly that children must respect the value of their parents' teaching, or their lives will be lacking the lavish blessing of God's mercy.

> Use the Bible as your guideline when you teach your children.

Teach your children when they are young what the Bible says. If they have the teaching in front of them, they will learn to understand the blessings that come from God through you. Use the Bible as your guideline when you teach your children. When they are older, pray for God to work his words into their hearts and enable them to obey. Pray more than you try to convince them, because God knows best how to reach them. Trust that God will ultimately see to their willingness and guide them.

Teach your children how smart it is to obey God. Pray with them and teach them what the Bible says, and let God work in their hearts.

I am sure that neither death, nor life, nor angels, nor ruling spirits, nothing now, nothing in the future, no powers, nothing above us, nothing below us, nor anything else in the whole world will ever be able to separate us from the love of God that is in Christ Jesus our Lord.

ROMANS 8:38–39 NCV

The Power of Love

You love your children deeply. You would do anything for them, and separation from them is painful. If anyone hurt your child, you would turn into a ferocious mama lion of protection. Poets have written eloquently about the love of a mother for her children, because it is such a great love. If you can imagine, as fiercely as you love your children, God loves you even more.

God's deep and unfathomable love for you is at the very heart of your relationship with him, and he wants you so completely sure of his love that your faith can be strong and resilient. These words compellingly convince you that there is nothing you could think of or experience that would change how God feels about you.

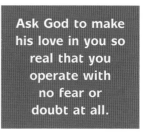

Ask God to make his love in you so real that you operate with no fear or doubt at all.

Knowing God's love in such a clear way makes everything different. You are more secure in your relationships with others because you know it does not matter if people do not like you. When your children are mad at you, you know that God still cares. When bad things happen in your life, you know that God still loves you and that he will show you a way through them. Ask God to make his love in you so real that you operate with no fear or doubt at all.

God's love for you can't be contained, changed, or stopped. God's love will never fail you, so walk through your days in confidence.

Neither is man independent of woman, nor woman independent of man, in the Lord.

1 CORINTHIANS 11:11 NKJV

God's Plan

Mothers and fathers parent differently. Sometimes one parent may be the disciplinarian, and the other one more relaxed. At times the differences may cause friction, but at other times you can see the benefit of having another point of view. Mothers who raise their children without a partner often struggle to fill both roles. God, because he is good and always compassionate, understands every situation you face.

God, in his perfect plan, created differences between genders to enable parents to fit together his way. In his plan, mothers and fathers cannot completely take each other's roles in life, and they cannot function best without each other. In his letters to the church of Corinth, Paul taught this in plain language, encouraging husbands

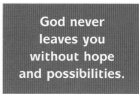

God never leaves you without hope and possibilities.

and wives, mothers and fathers, to need each other so children end up raised in a well-balanced manner.

When one parent cannot fill his role, or when a mom is raising her children alone, God is gracious and will step in to create that balance needed. He can give you the wisdom and strength to go beyond your traditional role of parenting, and he can provide healthy male influences for your children, if needed, as they grow. God never leaves you without hope and possibilities. His plan is perfect, but he is perfectly able to make it happen, regardless of the circumstances.

Children need what mothers and fathers give. Appreciate the differences God created, and trust him to provide the balance needed in your family.

Clean the slate, God, so we can start the day fresh! Keep me from stupid sins, from thinking I can take over your work.

PSALM 19:13 MSG

God Gives You Do-Overs

The effects of bad choices strike as quickly as lightning bolts. If you make a blunder, you may feel stupid. One unintentional mistake can turn an otherwise uneventful day into an embarrassing mess. You affect others by forgetting the promise of cupcakes for your child's class, or by not remembering a commitment that was important to your family. Afterward, you wish you could avoid mistakes like that, but they seem to keep happening.

Thankfully, God has an unlimited ability to forgive you for the kinds of blunders that disappoint and hurt others. God has a perfect plan for this. You can go to him in complete honesty each time you choose badly and ask for a fresh start. What a relief! When you pray and ask, he will protect you from making mistakes and from doing what you know is wrong.

> God has an unlimited ability to forgive you for the kinds of blunders that disappoint and hurt others.

Only God can keep you from falling into careless sin, or from carrying the weight of sinful mistakes. Believe that God can strengthen you, open your eyes, and keep you from things that may hurt your children or others. God wipes the slate clean and energizes you again to start fresh. Acknowledge his control in your life, and thank him every morning for a brand-new start.

Remember that no mistake is too bad for God to turn around. Let him forgive you of all your failures and shortcomings, and start every day free from regret.

Keep your lives free from the love of money, and be satisfied with what you have. God has said, "I will never leave you; I will never forget you."

HEBREWS 13:5 NCV

Trust in God

Many people believe that money is the solution to all problems. Even though the motto printed on money says, "In God We Trust," most people believe that properly invested money will ease their future woes. With enough money, so the thinking goes, you should be able to find relaxation, better health, a happier life, and the end to most of your troubles. Your children start catching this idea as they grow, but the premise is simply not true.

It is easy to become entangled in the quest to make more money, but you know the truth that the more you make, the more things demand your money. It is never enough. Raising children opens the door to expenses you never dreamed of in medical bills, orthodontics, school costs, and a host of other items. And if extra money does come in, you know how often an unexpected expense pops up to claim it.

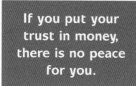

If you put your trust in money, there is no peace for you.

The Bible does not say to get rid of your money or try not to use money at all. Instead, the Bible says to rid yourself of the importance of money in your life. If you put your trust in money, there is no peace for you. Instead, base your trust, comfort, and security in the unfailing, always present God, who knows your need and provides what your family needs.

Trust God to provide all the needs of your family. Focus on him and on his faithfulness, and be happy with what you have.

God's riches are very great, and his wisdom and knowledge have no end! No one can explain the things God decides or understand his ways.

ROMANS 11:33 NCV

More Than You Can Imagine

How big is the sun? Why do birds sing? When is it dark in China? When your children are small, you must answer questions about everything that causes them wonder. You can tell them why dogs bark, or how the stars move from place to place, but there will always be questions you cannot answer. Children take the unanswered ones in stride and never seem too concerned when a mystery remains.

You face a mystery in your own life. No matter how hard you try, you cannot completely understand or explain God.

In fact, the more you learn, the more you see that God is so gracious, so perfect, so wise, and so complex that you will never grasp his entirety. He has always been, and will always be. He is immeasurable and is everywhere at

> **No matter how hard you try, you cannot completely understand or explain God.**

once. He never sleeps, and he hears every single prayer uttered by every person. When you grasp even a part of this, there is no response appropriate except absolute awe.

God sees your questions the way you see your children's questions. It is okay to have questions remain unanswered about God. God knows he is unsearchable and more than you can ever comprehend, and that makes it all the more amazing that he loves you. Teach your children that God is sometimes a mystery, and that it is wonderful.

Know that God is deep and rich, beyond human understanding, and yet he loves you as if you were his only child. Treasure that assurance of his love.

Your Father knows the things you have need of before you ask Him.

MATTHEW 6:8 NKJV

God Already Knows

Your little girl comes into the kitchen with her sweaty hair pushed up in the front. Swinging in the summer heat made her very hot. With her sweet lisp, she stammers as she tries to ask you for a glass of water. You know what she wants, but she is so precious, you wait until she finally gets out the request, and then you hand her a cold glass of water with a kiss. She trusts you and knows that you will provide her need for water because you love her. She never doubts it.

In Matthew 6, one short verse lets you know that God is looking at you with such affection that he knows everything you need before you even ask. His heart melts when he thinks of you, just as yours does for your child. He does not wait until you pray just right, or until you do anything to prove what you need. He loves you much more

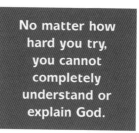

No matter how hard you try, you cannot completely understand or explain God.

than you love your children, and he sees your precious trust in him when you pray. You delight him!

Approach God in great trust, just as your children confidently approach you when they need something. Know that he will never let you down, and even needs that seem delayed are needs that will come when he knows the timing is perfect. God promises to give you everything you need. Trust him, and let your prayers be sweet words to his ears as you wait contently for his provision.

God knows what you need before you ask; simply go to him in childlike trust.

If you walk in My statutes and keep My commandments, and perform them, then I will give you rain in its season, the land shall yield its produce, and the trees of the field shall yield their fruit.

LEVITICUS 26:3–4 NKJV

A Plentiful Harvest

When your child first brought home a crushed paper cup from school, filled with dirt and a bean seed, he learned that with the proper care and plenty of sunshine and water his seed would grow into a plant that could produce more beans. By planting the seed and caring for it, he could produce a tiny harvest. He learned the law of nature that says by doing one thing you will get a predictable result. Plant a seed carefully, and grow a plant.

You plant seeds of a different kind when you obey God, and you receive a predictable harvest accordingly. If you plant obedience to God's teachings and laws, blessing will grow in your children's lives. Teaching your children to obey God's laws plants those seeds in their lives, which will grow a crop of right living and blessing as you nurture and care for them.

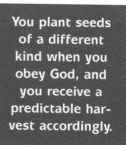

You plant seeds of a different kind when you obey God, and you receive a predictable harvest accordingly.

As a mother, you can see the connection between obeying God and receiving the good things he wants to give you. Plant your children firmly in the knowledge of God's laws and the practice of doing them. God will give them what they need to flourish. Teach them and pray for them. And one day, you will see a great pile of good things they have produced from the generosity and loving care of God.

Teach your children to do gladly what God wants, and you do the same. Then watch them burst into bloom with promise!

Children, do what your parents tell you. This is only right. "Honor your father and mother" is the first commandment that has a promise attached to it, namely, "so you will live well and have a long life."

EPHESIANS 6:1–3 MSG

Live Well and Live Long

"Because I said so!" How many times have you used that answer when your children challenge what you say? It rarely satisfies them, and you know the next time it comes up, chances are, they will challenge you again. It seems children never tire of questioning your authority as a mother. If they only understood how important it is, you know they would be much more agreeable.

God understands the challenge of raising respectful children. In Exodus 20, God gave a commandment especially for children, which shows how important he regards children's honoring their parents with obedience. It is the only one of the Ten Commandments God gave to people that has a promise with it. According to the Bible, children will have a good life when they obey this commandment.

> Let your children see your example of showing respect for your parents.

Know that when you patiently insist that your children treat you with honor and respect, and when they obey what you say, you are doing what pleases God. Pray and ask God to help you teach them, and to help your children be able to obey. God will back you up on this. Let your children see your example of showing respect for your parents. That example will reinforce everything you are trying to teach them.

Teach your children God's command when they are young, and show the respect you have for your own parents. Then their lives will be good.

L̲et patience have its perfect work, that you may be perfect and complete, lacking nothing.

JAMES 1:4 NKJV

Are We There Yet?

Children riding in a car on a long trip present the perfect picture of impatience. "Are we there yet?" "She's touching me!" "When can we get out?" You know in all the fussing, they miss many of the interesting things available to see along the way. As the mediator in their fighting, you also miss many of the things you would have enjoyed experiencing.

God made you as you are, and he knows that patience doesn't always come easily. Your children can bring out your impatience in remarkable ways, causing anything from edginess to full-out anger when they fight, refuse to obey, or resist your discipline. But patience is not just a condition for which to aim. Patience is something that will work exceptional good in you.

> Patience is not just a condition for which to aim. Patience is something that will work exceptional good in you.

You do not want to miss the good things God has for you on the journey of your life. If you fuss and chafe when you have to wait for answers to prayer, or for help with decisions, you may miss something God wants to use to enrich your life. You hear jokes about never asking for patience unless you want to go through more trouble, but if having patience increases what you can receive from God, it is a good thing. Ask away.

Welcome the chance to practice patience, knowing that God will bless your life with good things when you do.

Whoever listens to what is taught will succeed, and whoever trusts the LORD will be happy.

PROVERBS 16:20 NCV

Are You Listening?

When talking to your child, you know if he is listening to you. If his attention wanders and his eyes drift away from yours, you know you have lost his attention. Depending on what you were trying to say, he might miss out on a valuable lesson or a piece of advice. Later, he will be sorry he missed it. He does not always immediately appreciate the benefits of your wisdom.

In much the same way, God knows when you are listening to him. If you do not learn from what he tells you, life will be much harder. Proverbs 16 clearly states the positive consequences for listening to God's instruction. God promises joy and good feelings of satisfaction when you hear and understand what he is trying to teach you.

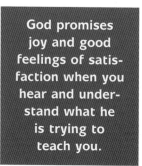

God promises joy and good feelings of satisfaction when you hear and understand what he is trying to teach you.

Instruction comes from God's words in the Bible, but also from teachers and pastors who understand God's ways and teach others. Instruction from a mature friend or a spouse is important to hear as well. When you have learned from God in any of these ways, you are then equipped to teach your own children the lessons you have learned. They, too, will know the joy of trusting in what is right. Ask God to help you hear what he wants you to learn.

Hear what God is saying to you and learn from it. You will experience delightful joy when you trust in him.

Nothing gives me greater joy than to hear that my children are following the way of truth.

3 JOHN 4 NCV

You have need of endurance, so that after you have done the will of God, you may receive the promise.

HEBREWS 10:36 NKJV

Hang On

Your children display great persistence. They ask the same question dozens of times, knowing that if they keep on going, you may wear down and say yes. They can hang on to a dream or hope for a long time, believing that they will see it happen. They just do not give up easily.

Can you remember praying about something for what seemed like an eternity, only to lose so much steam before

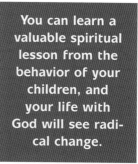
the answer came that you felt like quitting? Or do you remember times when you knew God wanted you to do something, and you couldn't make yourself do it? You can learn a valuable spiritual lesson from the behavior of your children, and your life with God will see radical change.

> **You can learn a valuable spiritual lesson from the behavior of your children, and your life with God will see radical change.**

You need a childlike persistence in order to enjoy the blessings God has promised. Just don't give up! If you obey God's commands and trust him, you will dig in and refuse to give up your belief that God will do what he says he will. Write down your prayers if it is hard to remember them, and make a note of the date of the answers. You will encourage yourself to have even greater faith, and you will have something solid to show your children when you teach them how to hang on with God.

Stick to your faith and prayers, no matter what things look like. God's promises come to those who believe enough to hold on.

Do not think like children. In evil things be like babies, but in your thinking you should be like adults.

1 CORINTHIANS 14:20 NCV

Growing Wise in God's Ways

Young children are delightfully unaware of the larger world around them. They enjoy their family and their toys, and are unconcerned with anything else. Their innocence is charming. As they grow older, they begin to question and struggle to understand a world bigger and more challenging than their own home.

God uses the innocence of children as an example of right living for you. First Corinthians 14:20 counsels you to be like an innocent baby with regard to anything evil. You cannot pretend bad things don't exist, but you can have no part of them. Be as far away from sinful actions and practices as your little ones are. This will guard you and your family from harm.

Just as it would be unnatural for a child to continue in babyish behavior as she grows, so you won't be naive in your spiritual understanding. Paul emphasized the importance of growing up in your faith and being a mature follower of God. Your thinking becomes adult. Make a habit of praying and reading the Bible, as well as enjoying a positive connection to others who are doing the same. Then model that growth and wisdom for your children, and they will follow in your steps.

> **Make a habit of praying and reading the Bible, as well as enjoying positive connection to others who are doing the same.**

⸻

Be innocent of evil things, and grow up in your understanding. God wants you wise and mature in your faith.

"**My** grace is sufficient for you, for My strength is made perfect in weakness." Therefore most gladly I will rather boast in my infirmities, that the power of Christ may rest upon me.

2 CORINTHIANS 12:9 NKJV

No Need to DIY

"I can do it myself." Surely you have heard that before, from little tykes determined to tie their own shoelaces or button their own coats. They want to show you that they can do things without help. They will keep trying until they get it. If you try to rush them along by helping, they protest.

Most people continue into adulthood with that same kind of determination to be self-sufficient, so it is not easy to give in to God's ways. A verse in 2 Corinthians gives the perfect solution for the endlessly tiring job of trying not to need anyone. God shines in your weakness. He shows his strength and greatness every time anyone is willing to invite him in.

> Do not tell God you can do it yourself. Ask for his help and watch him partner with you.

You would love it if your children would allow you to help them when the task they are trying is impossibly hard for them. Eventually, they may ask for help. Before *you* suffer long, stop and ask God to step in to do what you cannot. You will have marvelous rest and joy as you watch him do things in your life that you know would have worn you down. Do not tell God you can do it yourself. Ask for his help and watch him partner with you.

⸺⁘⸺

There is strength in being weak—God's strength! Let God step in and do what you cannot.

Lᴏʀᴅ our Lord, your name is the most wonderful name in all the earth! It brings you praise in heaven above. You have taught children and babies to sing praises to you.

Pꜱᴀʟᴍ 8:1–2 ɴᴄᴠ

Sing Out Praise

Little ones seem to know a secret. Babies start kicking and smiling with joy for no apparent reason. Little children are awestruck by things in nature that adults walk by without noticing. They see everything as fresh and exciting. When they know about God, they are quick to praise him in wonder and awe for the exciting world around them.

Praise from little children tickles the heart of God because of their sincerity and innocence. In Psalm 8, the response to God from little ones is cited as evidence of the awesome nature of God seen in the earth. Imagine the enemies of God stunned because even tiny children can sense the power and majesty of God and respond freely. Adults are so careful not to act unsophisticated that it is easy for people to miss the freedom and delight that please the heart of God in worship.

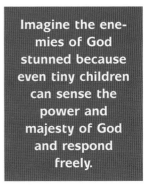

Imagine the enemies of God stunned because even tiny children can sense the power and majesty of God and respond freely.

Become like a child again and lose your inhibitions. Sing freely around your house; dance with joy before God. Be lost in wonder as you see all that God has created and all he has done. Get on your knees if need be to see things as your children see them. Delight them as you encourage the adoration that comes so naturally from them for God. Please God, and enjoy the pleasure you get from doing so.

Cut loose and enjoy the goodness of God! Tell him so in words of praise, freely and without shame. Become like a little one in your joy.

God's Spirit is right alongside helping us along. If we don't know how or what to pray, it doesn't matter. He does our praying in and for us, making prayer out of our wordless sighs, our aching groans.

ROMANS 8:26 MSG

Don't Know What to Say?

Few moms feel adequate when they pray. The Bible says to pray at all times, but you do not always know what to say, or you feel hampered when your choice of words does not express what your heart feels. Motherhood effectively brings you to a place where you know you must pray—for any one of the hundreds of situations requiring the prayerful love of a mother in your children's lives. And just as many situations need prayer that you do not know about.

There is a confidence-inspiring answer to the agony of not knowing the best words to use to pray for every situation: God gives you his Spirit to help you pray. You have an insider to help you know exactly how to talk to God.

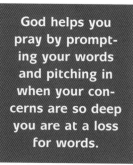

God helps you pray by prompting your words and pitching in when your concerns are so deep you are at a loss for words.

What a marvelous promise. God helps you pray by prompting your words and pitching in when your concerns are so deep you are at a loss for words. How more perfect could his help be? When your concerns for your children and their future weigh heavily on you, God helps you pray. When someone is sick and you are worried, God helps you pray. Nothing escapes his notice. Thank God for the help of his Spirit, and feel free to pray every time you are concerned for anything.

⁓🙏

Pray about everything, with words or without. Trust that God's Spirit is right alongside you, helping you cover all your concerns with a blanket of prayer.

You shall love the LORD your God with all your heart, with all your soul, and with all your strength.

DEUTERONOMY 6:5 NKJV

All You've Got

Your children love you unconditionally. You love them just as deeply and completely. The relationship between mother and children is an unbreakable kind of love, a deep bond, and is difficult to sever. Even when children enter young adulthood and act more standoffish, the bond still stands. Your life was changed when you first had children, and you learned to love in this new and compelling way.

Deuteronomy 6:5 gives a command for you to have a bond of love for God above everything else that you currently know, and to give God first place in your life. That means unconditional, absolute devotion to your Creator, which is unaffected by anything that happens in your life. Just as your child, created in your womb, is totally dependent on you, so you are dependent on God. Created by him in mysterious detail, he loved you before you even knew him.

> Loving God with all your heart means not letting other things crowd him out of your affection and devotion.

Loving God with all your heart means not letting other things crowd him out of your affection and devotion. Loving him with all your soul means choosing to set your emotional response toward God first and foremost, and loving him with all your might means giving him all you have in terms of effort and priority and praise. Following the command of God to love him this way will set everything else right in your life.

~*~

Go ahead—make God first in your life, and love him with all that you have. Watch your life fall into order when you put him in first place.

This is what the LORD says: "Stand where the roads cross and look. Ask where the old way is, where the good way is, and walk on it. If you do, you will find rest for yourselves."

JEREMIAH 6:16 NCV

Who Has the Answer?

Everywhere you turn, experts tell you how to raise your children and live your life. Never before have so many promoted *the* answers in self-help. Their advice shouts from television and magazine covers to tell you how to fix bad feelings, come out on top of child-rearing problems, and get rid of guilt and stress. The messages come from so many sources that the answers become jumbled and unclear, only to be replaced by new expert answers the next week.

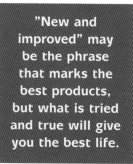

Raising children is a tough but rewarding job. Challenging situations can leave you wondering what answer is the right one. Only one source of help, though, is timeless, and only one path leads to peace. "New and improved" may be the phrase that marks the best products, but what is tried and true will give you the best life.

> "New and improved" may be the phrase that marks the best products, but what is tried and true will give you the best life.

God's ways are perfect for you. His words hold the key to any human condition, because he knows you best. You can hear perfect wisdom from your perfect Creator. God's truth has never changed, and that truth is completely relevant to your life. By asking God in prayer to show you what you need for the situations you face, you can find the one way proved to be the best—his path of help and rest.

Only God has the right answers for every situation. The same truths from centuries ago apply to your life today.

Let us hold fast the confession of our hope without wavering, for He who promised is faithful.

HEBREWS 10:23 NKJV

Willing to Wait

The best things in life are worth waiting for. Think of what you have waited for—the nine long months you waited for the promise of a new baby, or a long waiting period for the adoption of your child. In either case, the wait stretched on and on because of your anticipation of the baby you would hold in your arms. Deep down inside you knew there were no guarantees, and worry may have entered your mind as you waited.

Sometimes promises in life seem uncertain. Friends cannot always come through with the help they vowed to give you. Jobs may not last, and spouses sometimes do not follow through with what they vowed. You try to count on the promises you have had from others, but you know realistically that people are not perfect. You know that

> You can count on the hope you have in God, even if everything around you falters.

even the promises you speak to your children may later be hard to keep.

Only God can give an absolute and unbreakable promise into which you can pour all your hope. God made a way for you to come to him, and you always have access. You can count on the hope you have in God, even if everything around you falters. Teach your children that God never fails, and know that even if you have to wait, he *will* come through for you.

Hang on to the promises of God. They are unbreakable. You can count on God when nothing else is certain.

God is working in you to help you want
to do and be able to do what pleases him.

PHILIPPIANS 2:13 NCV

Pleasing God

When your children are young, they try hard to make
you proud of them. Their fumbling efforts to do the right
thing come from earnest desires to make you happy. You
know they cannot accomplish tasks themselves, so you
make it possible for them to succeed with well-placed and
subtle help using your wisdom as a mom.

When you follow God, he calls you his child and loves
you as his. As much as you wish to ensure your child's suc-

cess because you love her, God's desire for *your* spiritual success is more than you can imagine. God's earnest wish for you is to be successful in your faith, even to the point that he helps you have the desire to make him happy.

> **When you try to please God, he will work his power in you to give you every advantage.**

When you try to please God, he will work his power in you to give you every advantage. He helps you make right choices and do what the Bible tells you. He draws you to read the Bible and to pray. He will even make changes in you to remove things that would block your path to him. Knowing you have this assistance from God himself, you can rest assured that although you make mistakes, he will work to turn your failures into growth and maturity. Allow God to work in your life, and you will make him very glad.

Tell God you want his help doing the right thing. He will give you the power to want to obey him and will turn your efforts into his joy.

All this is from God. Through Christ, God made peace between us and himself, and God gave us the work of telling everyone about the peace we can have with him.

2 CORINTHIANS 5:18 NCV

Being a Peacemaker

Moms know siblings often fight and argue whenever they have the chance. Children without brothers or sisters will even argue with parents or neighborhood children. Fighting disrupts the tranquillity of your home in an instant, and even though you want with all your heart to put a stop to it, discord seems unavoidable.

God's message through his Son, Jesus, is that he sent peace to the world. As a follower of Christ, you can have tranquillity in your life. It comes through your relationship with God. When you pray and let him change your attitude to be more like his, you find out how to avoid contention. A peaceful home begins when you exemplify God's truth at home. Saying "I'm sorry, will you forgive me?" is powerful and can mend many family disagreements.

> As a follower of God, you can have tranquility in your life.

You can be a peacemaker in your own home. Teach your children that reconciliation is the key to peace with God and with others. Teach them to admit their mistakes and to ask forgiveness. Teach them to recognize their own bad attitudes and to ask God for help with them, and your home will be a better place. Then your children will be able to take the message of reconciliation everywhere they go.

Learn how to find harmony with one another and with God. Make your family's habit one of practicing reconciliation wherever they go.

Whoever listens to you listens to me, and whoever refuses to accept you refuses to accept me. And whoever refuses to accept me refuses to accept the One who sent me.

LUKE 10:16 NCV

God Stands Beside You

When friends turn against your child or your child loses a coveted position on a team in school, your heart aches for her. Rejection hurts. For years, you can still remember the boy who turned you down for the dance or the company who refused to hire you for your first job. Rejection happens in situations that seem unjust, despite all your efforts to do the right thing, and that really hurts. Making right choices

takes effort, but doing so doesn't ensure that others will respond to you positively.

God cares about every hurt that comes into your life. When you and your children suffer pain trying to do things God's way, God cares. An incredible reassurance is that God represents you in your dealings with others. Rejection actually loses its sting when it comes your way. Can you fathom God caring about you and your children so much that he takes the rejection instead of you?

> Can you fathom God caring about you and your children so much that he takes the rejection instead of you?

God does indeed care about the pain of relationships that affect your life and the lives of your children. His promise reassures you that you do not bear the effects alone. Your rejection becomes his problem. You can take the things that hurt you to God in prayer and ask him to heal your heart. He stands up for you and protects you because you are his.

—

God cares so much about your rejection that he takes it on himself. Let him stand up for you and heal your pain.

She watches over the ways of her household, and does not eat the bread of idleness. Her children rise up and call her blessed; her husband also, and he praises her.

PROVERBS 31:27–28 NKJV

Busy and Blessed

Where does a mom go to retire? Nowhere! Moms do not have retirement plans. While the thought may sound appealing when you finally take a few minutes out of a busy day to relax, you know you would not trade raising your family for any other life. Whether you work outside the home or stay at home with children, you have an important job that no one else can do the same way.

Raising children is incredibly important. Proverbs 31 describes a virtuous woman—one highly commended by God and by others—and that woman keeps busy taking care of her family. To see child rearing respected as important lets you know how important God regards what you do. A

You have an important job that no one else can do the same way.

mother who works diligently and cares for her family well is the one who will end up receiving praise for her efforts.

As a mother, you can know joy in your duty. Accepting the role of mom as honorable is one step toward joyful fulfillment. Being willing to give it your all is another way to be satisfied with being a woman raising children. Know that God sees all that you do and values every bit of the care you pour into your family. Whether anyone applauds your efforts or not, God values the love and attention you pour on your family.

What you do is of great worth. Even in your busyness, know that God appreciates you and so does your family.

Lᴏʀᴅ our Lord, your name
is the most wonderful name
in all the earth! It brings
you praise in heaven above.
You have taught children
and babies to sing praises
to you.

Psᴀʟᴍ 8:1–2 NCV

He leads me beside the still waters. He restores my soul.

PSALM 23:2–3 NKJV

Refreshment from God

Painters often depict images of quiet streams of water, tall trees, and sunlight dappling through the leaves. When you see paintings like that, you imagine rest and relaxation and can almost hear the tiny noises the water makes. If you have visited parks and walked beside gently flowing water, you felt tension draining out of your body as you watched and listened.

God paints the same picture to tell you the kind of rejuvenation only he can do in you. In Psalm 23, he uses the imagery of quiet water to describe a place where you become refreshed from the inside out. This renewing is vital for a mother who cares for others every day. God promises to address the worn-down and worn-out parts inside you by pouring new life into you.

> You can let the tiredness you feel flow out, pray, and receive a fresh flow of energy and focus.

This refreshing is for you. You need it. Life often brings rapids and white water into your life, and that leaves little time to rest and quench your thirst. When you pray, picture the quiet place God takes you. Let the tiredness you feel flow out, pray, and receive a fresh flow of energy and focus. In the quiet place where you meet with God, recharge with his peace and love. Linger there and go back to the demands of your life filled once again.

~⦿

Make time to meet with God in prayer. In that quiet place, let him refresh your soul and give you new life.

Correct your children, and you will be proud; they will give you satisfaction.

PROVERBS 29:17 NCV

Love Enough to Discipline

Delightful children are well-behaved children. You notice when the children of others act well, particularly when you wait in doctors' offices or in long lines at the post office, places guaranteed to try the patience of young ones. Parents of children who do not behave suffer embarrassment when their children fuss and ignore their attempts to correct them. You know times when you felt the same way about your children's public manners.

Discipline takes time and energy. Discipline requires that you drill the same rules of conduct over and over into your children, until they naturally fall into right behavior as they grow older. God understands just what children need, and the Bible states it clearly. Parental guidance is never an option. By following God's standards, you can have a peaceful household.

> Teach your children to obey God and obey you, and watch what God will do in their lives.

Children need consistent, firm training. With God's help, you can do this consistently enough that your children learn to feel safe and know their boundaries. The Bible tells you to train your children, and that God will bless them. Teach your children to obey God and obey you, and watch what God will do in their lives. Your children will bring peaceful rest to your home as their behavior improves. Your heart will be glad when your children choose to obey.

Lay out guidelines of discipline for your children, and stick to them. Loving discipline makes for well-behaved kids and allows God to bless them.

You wives should yield to your husbands. Then, if some husbands do not obey God's teaching, they will be persuaded to believe without anyone's saying a word to them. They will be persuaded by the way their wives live. Your husbands will see the pure lives you live with your respect for God.

1 PETER 3:1–2 NCV

Disagree Respectfully

While raising children, disagreements will arise with others. It may be that differences of opinion regarding rearing and disciplining children occur with your husband or your extended family or your friends. You will experience disagreements with your children as they reach the teen years. When spiritual differences also exist in your family, the chance for disagreement grows.

If you are married, the relationship you have with your spouse is the biggest test of respect you will face. How you deal with varying opinions sets the tone of your household and affects your attitude as a mother. If you trust God and the promise he gives, you have a way to honor God and keep a peaceful home: hold your tongue when you most want to insist that your belief is right.

> You have a way to honor God and keep a peaceful home: hold your tongue when you most want to insist that your belief is right.

God knows how difficult this can be. But you are simply to live out what you believe with no preaching, lectures, or endless arguments. If you believe God, respect your husband, and are genuine in your faith, God will work in your whole family. Your faith speaks volumes, and you will have a peaceful heart as a mother. Respect causes more respect to grow, and you model that attitude for your children. The way you respond will benefit your whole family.

—✺

When disagreements come, deal with them using great respect. Your children learn the value of respect by watching your behavior.

Remember to observe the Sabbath day by keeping it holy. Six days a week are set apart for your daily duties and regular work, but the seventh day is a day of rest dedicated to the LORD your God. On that day no one in your household may do any kind of work.

EXODUS 20:8–10 NLT

A Day to Rest

Children love to hear the story of Creation. They recite all the facts and tell how God created the whole earth in one week. Nothing is too difficult for God. His magnificent acts and wonderful deeds are described in the Bible but still hard to imagine. Picture the Red Sea parting and leaving a path of dry land, or the sun stopping in the sky for a time. God is limitless.

God commands that you do as he did, however, and rest on the seventh day of the week. God had no need for rest, but after creating all that exists, he decreed that the seventh day be set aside for rest. As a mom without enough hours in the day as it is, a day devoted just to rest seems like an extravagance, but it is more than rest. To keep the day God's way, it needs to be a time of reflecting on what is good and right.

> When you take a day for remembering how special God is, you will find that the remainder of your week becomes more productive.

God also asked that the day be dedicated to him, not a day for running errands and doing things for your own enjoyment, but for doing things that honor him. When you take a day for remembering how special God is, you will find that the remainder of your week becomes more productive. Who knows—you will probably enjoy the company of your family more than you could imagine!

Set one day aside to reflect on God and the good things you share as a family. These thoughts will bless the rest of your week.

I prayed for this child, and the LORD answered my prayer and gave him to me.

1 SAMUEL 1:27 NCV

An Answer to Prayer

A child sometimes tosses out careless words when she doesn't get her own way. Many children have hurtfully shouted "I hate you!" at some time during a fit of anger. While you know they do not really mean it, careless words can be painful for a mom to hear. It's tough to hear those words directed at you and coming from your child. Those are the times when you remind yourself that your child is the fulfillment of your great longing.

Children come from God and are an answer to your prayers. The first chapter of 1 Samuel captures a prayer uttered by a mother in the Bible as she acknowledged that aside from the circumstances of her life, God gave her the child she had waited for. It is an awesome responsibility to raise a child, and the responsibility lasts a lifetime, but the joy is tremendous.

It is an awesome responsibility to raise a child, and the responsibility lasts a lifetime, but the joy is tremendous.

Remember that God gave you this child. You longed for her and prayed for her. Even when your child is disrespectful or rejects you with her words, remember that God placed her in your care for a purpose. Knowing there is purpose for her life makes it easier to weather the upsets that come. Continue to pray and to hold on to the calling God has for you and your child.

No matter what your children say or do, remember that God gave them to you as an answer to prayer. Thank him for answered prayer.

Don't think I'm carrying around a list of personal grudges. The fact is that I'm joining in with your forgiveness, as Christ is with us, guiding us. After all, we don't want to unwittingly give Satan an opening for yet more mischief—we're not oblivious to his sly ways!

2 Corinthians 2:10–11 msg

Foil the Enemy

When trouble comes into your life, it is usually in an area you have difficulty getting under control. If anger is your weakness, things seem to pop up in your children to trigger a blowup. If impatience is your most common reaction, your children will push every button you have with slowness and lost shoes and coats. At times trouble seems closely matched to your sore spots.

If you follow Christ, you have an enemy. The enemy is the devil. He will watch for the areas that prove to be your undoing, and he will test you at those points with the temptation to lose your temper or speak harshly in impatience. By striking your weak areas, the

> **Forgive your children and allow them to forgive you.**

enemy hopes to discourage you and separate you from your connection to God and to others. But be smart and realize the tricks of the enemy.

One very common snare the enemy uses to bring trouble into your life occurs when you refuse to forgive someone who hurt you. Your refusal opens the door to a host of other troubles. When you forgive others, it breaks the hold the enemy has over you and allows God to work. Forgive your children and allow them to forgive you. Teach them to pinpoint their own weaknesses. They will learn to avoid being tripped up by the enemy as they watch you do the same.

Forgive others quickly and watch out for your weaknesses. Give the enemy no room to work.

Those who do not control themselves are like a city whose walls are broken down.

PROVERBS 25:28 NCV

Restrain Yourself

In ancient times, cities were vulnerable to attacks from outsiders and other threats, and so were protected by thick stone walls built around the city's edge. When those walls stayed strong and thick, enemies could not ravage the inhabitants of the settlement. Once a wall was down, the enemy could pour into the city like water and overtake them.

Your personal protection disintegrates with lack of self-control. Doing things that you should do because they are right are at the heart of this kind of resolve. Getting up on time, putting aside what you want to do, taking care of your children's needs before yours—all this requires self-control. Without self-control, life can get the best of you and leave you feeling washed over with failure and defeat when you give in to any temptation that leads to sinful attitudes or actions.

> **Without self-control, life can get the best of you and leave you feeling washed over with failure and defeat.**

Thanks to God, you do have a way to build up your walls. God, who tells you to have self-discipline, will give you greater control as you grow in him. The walls of protection grow as you become closer to God and as you pray and trust him to provide for all your needs as a mother of children. You are snug and secure within the walls of the self-control God develops in you to keep you and your family in a place of greater strength.

Practice self-restraint and watch as God makes you stronger. He will help you grow and make your family a stronger, safer place.

God called you to be free, but do not use your freedom as an excuse to do what pleases your sinful self. Serve each other with love.

GALATIANS 5:13 NCV

Serve Others

Because you are a mother, you care for your children. You may wish you had more time to yourself, but the needs of your family are greatest when you have young ones. Even though you love them, when you get up in the middle of the night for the sixth time with a child who has trouble sleeping, or when you lose time at work because you have a sick child, you may start to question what you are doing.

For a mom, your highest form of service occurs when you get up in the night with your children or help them when they are sick. You can serve them when you use most of your evening to help them with homework and your weekends to wash their clothes. Caring for your children shares the love of God with them.

> God calls you to find satisfaction in him, and to please him by thinking of others.

Take time to care for yourself. Good food, exercise, and rest help you to stay healthy and be your best. When you focus on serving others and sharing God's love with them, though, the acts of loving others keep you in healthy balance. God calls you to find satisfaction in him and to please him by thinking of others. Make loving God, loving your children, and loving one another top priorities in your life.

God made you free, so make good choices. Care for others and focus on loving them, and you will please God.

He who touches you touches the apple
of His [God's] eye.

ZECHARIAH 2:8 NKJV

You Are Cherished

You are God's precious creation. He imagined who you
would be before your conception. He imagined the way you
look, and he imagined the way you celebrate life. You are
precious enough that those who touch you will have to con-
tend with God. He cares so much that he is your protector,
your champion, and the One who looks out for your best
interests. He cares more for you than anyone else could.
Your welfare is his concern.

If you pattern yourself after your heavenly Father, you will see your children as the apples of *your* eye. You are the one who will stand for them when no one else will. You take action if someone tries to harm them, and you look out for their best interests. You can be their champion and cheerleader, and you can love them more than anyone else can.

> **Pattern yourself after your heavenly Father, and see your children as the apples of *your* eye.**

When you read the Bible, you cannot escape the fact that God cares for you and your children. You are chosen by God, and he will come to your rescue if you are harmed. Just as you protect and defend your children, God protects and defends you. God cherishes you; you can rest assured of his forever love. Your children learn of God's care for them by watching how you embrace his care and live as someone cherished by him.

Live as someone loved deeply by God. No one cares for you as he does. Teach your children to trust in his love.

Children are known by their behavior; their actions show if they are innocent and good.

PROVERBS 20:11 NCV

Actions Speak

When your children play at their friends' houses, you tell them to mind their manners and be on their best behavior. You tell them that if they act their best, they will be invited to visit and play again. They want to be welcomed by others, and so do you. Parents of your children's friends inevitably gauge how you have raised your children by the way they act in their homes. Their behavior is quite naturally a reflection on you.

As much as it matters to you what others think about your children, there is an even greater reason for children to learn to be obedient: others can judge your children's very character by their behavior. That gives strong motivation from God for you to train your children carefully and consistently. What begins as saying "Please" and "Thank you" culminates in a respect for God and for other people, their ideas, and their property.

> **What begins as saying "Please" and "Thank you" culminates in a respect for other people, their ideas, and their property.**

You know that your family's conduct in public speaks volumes to others. Ask God for his help to train your children to love God and to obey. Pray for them and with them every day. Use God's guidelines from the Bible when you discipline them. Let others see God's peace and happiness in your family. Your family's example to others is powerful.

Good behavior speaks of God's influence in your life. Let your training and your children's character shine to others.

Bless the LORD, O my soul, and forget not all His benefits.

PSALM 103:2 NKJV

Praise for God's Goodness

Children rarely realize all you do for them, and consequently they don't often show appreciation. You know how much you do for them, and you also know that you will continue even if they do not acknowledge it. Your joy overflows, though, when your children appreciate some of what you have done.

God asks you to remember all that he has done for you. Psalm 103 recounts an astonishing list of examples of his love and care for you. For every need you have, God has already provided a remedy. He heals you, provides materially and spiritually for you, gives your life purpose, pours his love on you, and restores your health and vitality. Much of this comes into your life without fanfare as a part of following him.

> For every need you have, God has already provided a remedy.

If you know what God has done for you, it overflows into blessing him with your words and thoughts. You cannot help bubbling over in appreciation for him when you recognize what your life would be like without his acts of grace and mercy. His promises are rich, full, and certain. When you thank God generously, blessings pour out on your children, as well. They learn of his love gifts and learn to let their mouths thank him. Your home will become a place of words that build up and commend as you think on all that is positive and good.

Recall all the good God gives you when you follow him. Give him praise for his love, and let good wash over your family as you do.

Open up before GOD, keep nothing back;
he'll do whatever needs to be done: He'll
validate your life in the clear light of day
and stamp you with approval at high noon.

PSALM 37:5–6 MSG

Give It All to God

What is most precious to you? Your children, your marriage, your dreams? Which of these hopes could you let go of if asked? You hold them all close to your heart because they are dear to you, but sometimes holding them so tightly allows worry and anxiety to tease your mind.

Psalm 37 gives you a bold challenge—to let go of the things you care most about, and to see what God will do with them. This is not as reckless a request as it sounds. It is a rich promise from a completely faithful God. Giving these things up to him means mentally and emotionally trusting him with every detail of your children's lives, your

> God will label your life with his mark of approval when you abandon yourself to his faithfulness and trust him.

marriage relationship, and the dreams you cherish. It means refusing to spend time worrying about what you can do to make them all succeed.

You cannot lose! God will label your life with his mark of approval when you abandon yourself to his faithfulness and trust him. He will work the details for you, so much better than you could even if you give it your best. Take that step, and throw yourself headlong into his care. Pray and dedicate your most beloved hopes and dreams to God, and watch what tremendous things he accomplishes.

Give everything over to God. Trust him with your most cherished hopes and watch what he accomplishes for you.

Correct your children, and you will be proud; they will give you satisfaction.

PROVERBS 29:17 NCV

It is not that we think we can do anything of lasting value by ourselves. Our only power and success come from God.

2 Corinthians 3:5 nlt

The Myth of Supermom

Supermom to the rescue! She handles everyone's life, remembers all important dates, fixes all problems, climbs the corporate ladder, and even has a clean house. She wears perfect makeup every day with perfectly coordinating superhero wear. Who does not want to be a supermom? She is praised as a legend of modern-day life.

This myth really damages women. You cannot do it all, or at least not for very long. Your health and mental strength will fare poorly if you try. The myth of supermom also blocks out the power of God in your life. Nothing works well that is driven just by you. The only true success in any endeavor comes from and is powered by God. Your children and other moms around you see where you put your confidence and learn by your example.

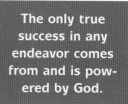

The only true success in any endeavor comes from and is powered by God.

Go to God in prayer with everything you have to do. Tell him you need him and his power each day. Ask him to show you what is important and what is not. Ask him for his wisdom and favor on your vocation as a mother. Be sure to let your daughter learn this by your example before she becomes a mother of her own children. Let God bring success to you in a way you couldn't do for yourself, and remember to thank him for it.

Do not depend on your own abilities, but trust completely in God's ability to give you success and wisdom as a mother. He can handle it all!

The only temptation that has come to you is that which everyone has. But you can trust God, who will not permit you to be tempted more than you can stand. But when you are tempted, he will also give you a way to escape so that you will be able to stand it.

1 CORINTHIANS 10:13 NCV

A Dependable Escape

Enticement strikes when you least expect it, whether it is double-fudge cake or the lure of a lazy afternoon when work has to be done. It is tempting to avoid the effort it takes to be consistent in discipline and correction. You know from experience how easy it is to give in to the sudden pull you feel at those times.

It is hard to imagine just saying no and refusing the urge to put off the hard work of parenting. But temptation leads to sin, and sin leads to serious breaks in your relationship with God and can influence your children. But there is hope. God provides you with a sure way out. You have a guarantee from him that your escape route will always be there.

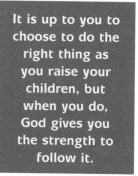

It is up to you to choose to do the right thing as you raise your children, but when you do, God gives you the strength to follow it.

God understands the power that lures you to wrongdoing. And he has placed a limit on what you will face. God knows the will power and the strength you have, but he also knows the emergency exit he has given you before trouble even comes your way. So when temptation comes, stop. Ask God in prayer to show you the way out, and then follow his leading. It is up to you to choose to do the right thing as you raise your children, but when you do, God gives you the strength to follow it.

No seduction has to pull you in. God already made a way out of the snare for you. Ask him to show you, then take that escape route.

Search me, O God, and know my heart; try me, and know my anxieties; and see if there is any wicked way in me, and lead me in the way everlasting.

PSALM 139:23–24 NKJV

The View Inside You

One special moment for you as a mother is the first time you see an ultrasound of your expected baby. You remember the concern you felt until you finally saw, with great relief, the little one floating peacefully, and you watched as the technician checked to make sure all was well. The science of ultrasound provides peace of mind when you are expecting and lets you know what to anticipate when your child is born.

Spiritually, there are times when you cannot know with certainty what is going on inside you. Most often, your spiritual side is healthy and working well, and you feel content in your role as a mother. Other times, you may be thinking about your circumstances in a way that brings worry or negative emotions. You may have an area of

> By asking God to show you what needs to change, you let him take an "ultrasound" of your heart.

sinful attitude in your life that you cannot see, and it affects you as a mother. It can affect the way you parent and rob you of peace of mind.

Psalm 139 is a beautiful prayer of permission for God to look inside at your spiritual condition. By asking God to show you what needs to change, you let him take an "ultrasound" of your heart. He sees things you cannot, and, further, he knows the best treatment for anything that is wrong. He will help you.

⌐∭⊙

Ask God to look inside your heart. He alone knows how to change you so you are spiritually healthy and content.

D o not worry about anything, but pray and ask God for everything you need, always giving thanks. And God's peace, which is so great we cannot understand it, will keep your hearts and minds in Christ Jesus.

PHILIPPIANS 4:6–7 NCV

The Attitude of Gratitude

A thoughtful thank-you note warms your heart like little else. When you have given someone a gift for her new baby or a special occasion, you truly understand her appreciation when she takes the time to express her thoughts in positive words. You may have tacked a special thank-you note on your mirror or desk to remember the kind words.

Thankfulness is an antidote to turn off worry. Sometimes you need to write down all you are thankful for and remind yourself of the good in your life. Philippians 4 tells you exactly why you should take the time to do this, for God planned all along to fill you with his peace when you let go of anxious thoughts and trust him with a heart filled with gratitude.

> Practice thankfulness in every area of your life, and you will find concerns melt away.

Practice thankfulness in every area of your life, and you will find concerns melt away. Let your children help make lists of thanksgiving with you, and you will be surprised at their points of view. Teach them the art of thankfulness, and they will likely teach you much in return. The more you can see and focus on what God has done for you and your children, the easier it will be to drop your worries and cares, and believe that God will take care of it all.

— ⁂

Make a list of all the things for which you give thanks, and review it daily. As you do, concerns and worry will simply fade away.

He gives children to the woman who has none and makes her a happy mother. Praise the LORD!

PSALM 113:9 NCV

Be Happy, Mama!

Children add joy to your life. Whether you gave birth to your children or adopted them into your heart, they filled a longing in your life. Children are also work. The load is heavy, and you carry the responsibility of raising children for many years, through every phase of their lives. Those parts of raising children loom large, and it is sometimes hard to enjoy your role.

Psalm 113 says that God gives children to mothers, and when he does the mother *is* happy. You can cooperate with God in achieving your happiness by accepting the role he has given you as a mother and working to be content in that role. If your focus is on raising your children with all the love and dedication you possess, and not on an endless quest to find fulfillment in other places, satisfaction will come. You *can* be truly happy raising children.

> If your focus is on raising your children with all the love and dedication you possess, and not on an endless quest to find fulfillment in other places, satisfaction will come.

Tell your children the story of how happy you were when you first held them in your arms. Describe that time, and let them know how much you love them. Remember what God has given you, and purposefully thank him for the gift of motherhood. When the negatives arise, focus on God and his gifts, and it will help you. Recapture the joy with determination and faith, and be a happy mother.

Be happy God made you a mother of children. Let him help you find true contentment and happiness in your role.

I know the thoughts that I think toward you, says the LORD, thoughts of peace and not of evil, to give you a future and a hope.

JEREMIAH 29:11 NKJV

God's Purpose for You

As you love and care for your children, you may wonder if you have a purpose in life that goes beyond wiping noses and feeding little ones. It is hard to see a future beyond raising your children, but it is there. God is thinking of you at all times, not only as his beloved child, but as a mother of children as well. Because he knows what he has planned, he is cheering you on as you walk out the steps in front of you.

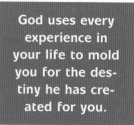

Jeremiah 29:11 is a beacon of light shining into your life as a mom. God assures you that no matter what your life looks like today, and no matter how limited you feel, he has a specific purpose for you. Raising children holds utmost importance for the future as you mold and shape part of the next generation. Your entire life matters to God, as well as every decision you make. Because it comes from God, your life is full of promise and significance.

> God uses every experience in your life to mold you for the destiny he has created for you.

God uses every experience in your life to mold you for the destiny he has created for you. Ask God to give you a picture of what he intends for your life. Your abilities and desires will bud and bloom as your children grow. Be open to whatever God has in mind.

Believe that your life is meaningful and has purpose in God's eyes. Be open to the direction he leads you as you grow in him.

$\mathbf{W}$ait for the LORD's help. Be strong and brave, and wait for the LORD's help.

PSALM 27:14 NCV

When You Are Waiting

Answers to prayer sometimes seem long in coming. But what do you do when you are waiting? Waiting does not always mean doing nothing. Adults waiting in lines do other tasks while they while away the minutes. Children fidget when they are waiting, and can be still only when you give them something else to do.

God decides when to act on your behalf, and you can trust he does not make mistakes. Because he is a perfect

God, his timing is also perfect. He not only sees today in your life, but he also knows what tomorrow will bring. Your children learn to trust that you know the best time to give them what they need. Just as they learn confidence in your judgment, you can learn to have confidence in God's perfect judgment. If time passes when you are praying for

> **Give God your prayers, and be willing to wait for the best time to see the answers come.**

something, God is waiting for the right time to act on your behalf.

In language that is clear but challenging, Psalm 27:14 encourages you to wait for God. Be brave and strong. Give God your prayers, and be willing to wait for the best time to see the answers come. He knows that you can have confidence enough to wait when you remember how trustworthy he has been for you in the past. God promises to help you, and he will never fail you.

—

Keep the faith when answers to prayer are long in coming. God never forgets, and he will answer when the time is just right.

A **happy heart is like good medicine.**

PROVERBS 17:22 NCV

Laugh and Be Healthy

Laughter is good for the soul. Doctors now find that chronically ill patients see improved immune response when exposed to laugh-inducing movies every day. Science agrees with the Bible on this point. Children act as if they must know this truth. They laugh hundreds of times a day, while some adults may find that days pass without a good belly laugh.

You may not always feel like laughing, for at times, motherhood is not funny. If you focus on your many responsibilities, motherhood seems serious indeed. Silliness sounds like a waste of time and too foolish for a grown woman. But the Bible says that laughter does your heart good, so imagine what it does for your growing children. Proverbs 17:22 is a prescription God gives you for better health and a happier disposition, and *this* Physician truly knows what is best for your whole family.

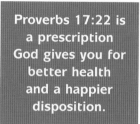

Proverbs 17:22 is a prescription God gives you for better health and a happier disposition.

Nothing is as beautiful as the sound of children laughing. The face of an adult who laughs more than she frowns every day is a refreshing sight. Notice how often your children laugh. Then join them, and take the time to tell silly jokes with your children. Read goofy books together, or dance a popular step to music after dinner. Watch old comedies with them, and have a good belly laugh. The tensions of the day will dissolve, you will bond together, and you will be happier as you become healthier.

Laugh and your children laugh with you. Be healthier, happier people as you use the "medicine" the Bible prescribes.

You, Lord, give true peace to those who depend on you, because they trust you.

Isaiah 26:3 NCV

A Place of Perfect Rest

In lifesaving classes, swimmers learn how to rescue a drowning person. A rescuer must be cautious, for a drowning person might flail against and push the rescuer under the water in their panic. The one saving the person in trouble has to grasp the struggling swimmer from behind and drag her to safety. Once relaxed in the rescuer's confident grip, the swimmer experiences security and relaxes, knowing she will not drown.

As a mom, you rarely relax. You do it all. You are everything for your children. You care for their physical needs, manage their time, plan their schedules, maintain their education, and wonder about their future. You balance everyone's needs in a constant juggling act.

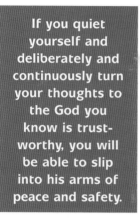

If you quiet yourself and deliberately and continuously turn your thoughts to the God you know is trustworthy, you will be able to slip into his arms of peace and safety.

God has a very specific place of rest, and it is just for you. That place is perfect peace. It is easy to keep thrashing and flailing, like the drowning swimmer, even when the place of calm surrounds you. If you quiet yourself and deliberately and continuously turn your thoughts to the God you know is trustworthy, you will be able to slip into his arms of peace and safety. His tranquillity is yours as long as your thoughts stay on him and not on the waves of stress that could sweep over you. He will safely carry you and give you calm no matter how rough the waters of your life.

Turn your thoughts continually to God. Do not give in to the stress around you, but trust and experience his quiet calm.

When the Spirit of truth comes, he will lead you into all truth. He will not speak his own words, but he will speak only what he hears, and he will tell you what is to come.

JOHN 16:13 NCV

To Tell the Truth

You teach your children to tell the truth. You work hard to show them the difference between the truth and a lie when they are young, and you work to keep them speaking the truth when they are older. It is important, too, for you to be an example of truth to them every day. Children quickly catch any inconsistencies in what they hear and see from their parents.

It also takes effort to keep a tight rein on your children as they learn to be truthful, and as you try to serve as a consistently good example. The only way to keep on top of the struggle and set a good example is to trust that God's Spirit will help you always head in the direction of truth. The Bible says that God is truth, and he will not allow you, as his own child, to be deceived

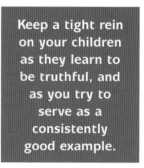

when you try to figure out what is right and what is wrong. He leads you.

Think about God and the help his Spirit gives you in understanding and finding the truth. Ask God to give you the strength to follow his truth in your words and actions. Lean on God for his help in teaching your children to walk in the path of truth. Pray for help to always speak the truth to others. And thank God that he will help you as you guide your children in truth.

Speak the truth, and model it for your children. Ask God to help you teach them truth. He will. He *is* truth.

If you've gotten anything at all out of following Christ, if his love has made any difference in your life, if being in a community of the Spirit means anything to you, if you have a heart, if you care—then do me a favor: Agree with each other, love each other, be deep-spirited friends.

PHILIPPIANS 2:1–2 MSG

Stick Together in God

On playgrounds, children play variations of red rover, where teams link arms together and an opposing team member runs as fast as he can and tries to break through the line. The unity of the children holds them together and makes them stronger than they would be standing apart.

A verse in the second chapter of Philippians begs you to have unity with others. Unity with your children makes a strong connection. God's Spirit in you and God's Spirit in them creates a place for the kind of deep relationship that will hold you and your children together. You can also find a common bond with other friends who are mothers. These friendships will strengthen your ability to parent as you share the joys and concerns common to motherhood. You can encourage and pray for one another from the place of unity.

> Work to agree on the key elements of faith and continually love and accept one another.

You live in a world that is sharply divided by religious doctrines, political beliefs, and many other issues. The sense of community described in Philippians is one with a depth of fellowship possible only if peaceable agreement is a conscious and deliberate goal. Work to agree on the key elements of faith and continually love and accept one another. You will see that strength comes from the like-mindedness you have and causes your relationships to be deeper and more enriching.

Be close and of the same mind with other followers of God. Your friendships will be deep and loving as you do.

You will not need to fight in this battle. Position yourselves, stand still and see the salvation of the LORD, who is with you.

2 CHRONICLES 20:17 NKJV

When You Cannot Fix Things

Have your children ever broken something valuable, like a vase or a lamp, and tried to fix it on their own? They might have used a glue that was wrong for china or glass, and made matters worse. They should have told you what they had done and let you choose a method of repair. Instead, they ruined the item by taking matters into their own hands. They meant well, but the outcome was poor.

There are situations God wants you to stop trying to fix. You need to let go of your desire to fix all the problems on your own that you encounter as you raise your children. You need to trust God enough to let go and let him handle the problem. He knows the solution for every problem you face.

> **The only way to know when to work on something and when to let go is to take everything to God.**

The only way to know when to work on something and when to let go is to take everything to God. Pray and ask him to show you when to give up your efforts, and to give to you the strength to do it. Once you see how much better God can fix difficult situations with your children, it gets easier and easier to give them to him. He knows the outcome before he starts, and he knows what he wants to do in their lives. Trust him to fight the battle for you.

God works for you and your children. Let him deal with situations you cannot fix, and watch him work on your behalf.

D̲on't make your children angry by the way you treat them. Rather, bring them up with the discipline and instruction approved by the Lord.

EPHESIANS 6:4 NLT

Anger Management from God

An epidemic of anger seems an inevitable part of life. The daily newspaper gives stories of the mistakes people make when they are angry when they drive or angry when they deal with others. Uncontrolled anger is the basis for many tragedies that pepper newspapers and news broadcasts. Angry people pop up everywhere. The modern lifestyle of rushing and stressing seems to encourage this kind of response.

It is crucial that anger not be a part of your child rearing. Harsh treatment or inconsistent discipline triggered by angry feelings breaks your children's spirits, which tears down the respect you have worked to build in them. They are defeated and their tenderness wilts. This warning is crystal clear in Paul's letter to the Ephesian church, when he warned parents to avoid anything that would foster resentment in their children.

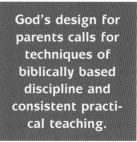

God's design for parents calls for techniques of biblically based discipline and consistent practical teaching.

God's design for parents calls for techniques of biblically based discipline and consistent practical teaching. He knows this is what makes strong moral children blossom under your care. If you have anger, pray and tell it to God. Ask him to change you and take away your temper. He will free you from seething, and he will replace your anger with peace as you raise your children. Then you will nurture your children in love and not frustration. Their spirits will bloom.

⚜

Confess feelings of anger to God, and ask him to remove them. He will show you how to respond to your children and have peace in your home.

In all the work you are doing, work the best you can. Work as if you were doing it for the Lord, not for people. Remember that you will receive your reward from the Lord, which he promised to his people. You are serving the Lord Christ.

COLOSSIANS 3:23–24 NCV

Who's Your Boss?

Do you feel scrutinized or judged by people around you? Whose opinion do you value in matters of child rearing? Your parents or in-laws have ideas about how your parenting is going: they might feel you let the children stay up too late or you put them to bed too early. You worry about your children's teachers in school: are you supporting their efforts? The pediatrician has questions too: are you keeping the children safe and well-fed? are you monitoring their television time?

You can be free from worry about the judgments of others. The way you parent is your role, but it is like a job, and like any other, you need be concerned about the opinion of only your boss. God is your boss, and he is the only One to whom you need to answer. What does he think about your parenting? How can you know?

> **When you pray and ask God for his wisdom and help, he gives you what you need to raise your children.**

The hard work and loving care you give your children are noticed by God. When you pray and ask God for his wisdom and help, he gives you what you need to raise your children. If you keep the lines of communication open to God through prayer, ask God for guidance, and are open to his voice, you will know if you are doing the right things for your children. Give the best effort you have, and trust God to give you the rest.

Remember that you answer to only God in your parenting. He oversees the job you do and gives you what you need for every situation.

Do not worry about anything, but pray and ask God for everything you need, always giving thanks.

PHILIPPIANS 4:6 NCV

No Worries at All

Being a mom makes it easy to worry. You wonder if your child dresses right, or if he eats enough vegetables. You want to know if he has good friends, or if he is learning what he should in school. Think of braces, college, and future marriages, and anxious thoughts can start gripping your heart. Can you adequately prepare him for his future happiness? Can you teach him what he needs to know?

God knows how vexing it can be to face the sometimes hair-raising challenges of raising children. Worry begins with caring, but there is a better way. Be a partner with God. If you hold on to concerns, your focus will be on things that could be problems rather than on the Problem Solver. Every problem grows larger if you look at it all the time.

> **Worry begins with caring, but there is a better way. Be a partner with God.**

Paul's advice in Philippians 4:6 beautifully describes the way to let God partner with you in parenting and in every aspect of life. By determining to praise God for every awesome characteristic that is his, those troubled and anxious thoughts will naturally transform into petitions of prayer you give to the one true and faithful God. When you give your troubled thoughts to God, you must leave them with him, for he is faithful to care for everything you leave in his capable hands.

Let your concerns become confident requests made to God, who always comes through for you. Let him work with you as you raise your children.

You will bear children as a vine bears grapes, your household lush as a vineyard, the children around your table as fresh and promising as young olive shoots. Stand in awe of God's Yes. Oh, how he blesses the one who fears GOD!

PSALM 128:3–4 MSG

The Promise of the Future

Children are a blessing. Psalm 128 beautifully describes how rich a blessing children are. Chances are good that you do not often imagine your home with children as a thick growth of olive or grape plants. In the psalm, the comparison was one of the most vivid to represent a home that is healthy, full of life, and full of great things in the future!

In many places, children are not viewed as precious. You have seen worn-out parents who are too tired to care, and children abandoned by those who brought them into the world. It is rare to see homes brimming over with "blessings" as they were in Bible times. Think what a tremendous opportunity God has given you to live in the way

> Think what a tremendous opportunity God has given you to live in the way that brings the most blessings.

that brings the most blessings, and to pray for those families who do not yet know.

The Bible says that not only are children a sign of God's blessing, but they represent promise. God views children as living, growing examples of hope to place in your life and around your table. The world will go on, and you are part of that process God allows to continue. His creative reproduction is powerful, and yet is given as a blessing to those who love him. What a tremendous gift to be allowed to participate in God's creation!

Believe and accept that children are a blessing, and thank God for the promise they represent in your life.

Do not worry about anything, but pray and ask God for everything you need, always giving thanks.

PHILIPPIANS 4:6 NCV